REVISED

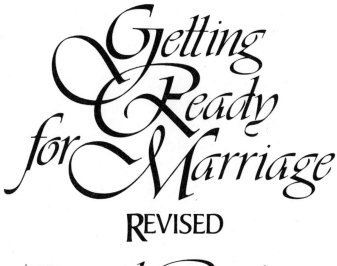

Getting Ready for Marriage

REVISED

David R. Mace

Abingdon Press
Nashville

GETTING READY FOR MARRIAGE, Revised

Copyright © 1972, 1985 by Abingdon Press

Library of Congress Cataloging in Publication Data

MACE, DAVID ROBERT.
  Getting ready for marriage.

  Bibliography: p.
  1. Family life education. 2. Marriage counseling.
I. Title.
HQ10.M325   1985   362.8'2   84-28320

ISBN 0-687-14136-2

MANUFACTURED BY THE PARTHENON PRESS AT
NASHVILLE, TENNESSEE, UNITED STATES OF AMERICA

I did not want one word of advice about Everett, myself, or the married state. I awaited marriage as revelation. I no more wanted a premarriage resume of what lay ahead than I want an inventory of Christmas presents before Christmas. I intended to launch into the state of Holy Matrimony unnourished by so much as a crumb of worldly knowledge; and I did so launch. The trouble was, Everett was launched in exactly the same manner. And what we were headed for was not so much a collision course as a complete miss.

Jessamyn West, A Matter of Time

Contents

Part One Preparation

Why It Is So Important

Part Two Yourselves

What You Bring to Each Other

Part Three Marriage

What You Must Do to Succeed

Preface

When marriage counselors reflect on their work and review in their minds the long procession of men and women in whose pain and perplexity they have been involved, they are at times overwhelmed as they realize the absurdity of our whole policy, or lack of policy, regarding marriage, the nuclear relationship upon which the human community is built.

We allow people to drift into this relationship, with all its maddening complexity, on pink clouds of romantic sentiment. We send them forth, after solemn ceremonies involving the blessing of religion and the hearty goodwill of relatives and friends, on a joint enterprise concerning which we have made no serious endeavor to enlighten them; and in which, as the dreary statistics make plain, a substantial number of them are doomed to fail.

We are prepared to spend considerable effort and money on the wedding, which is over in a few hours; yet we complacently leave to chance the outcome of the marriage, which is expected to last a lifetime. This has always seemed to me to be one of the most dramatic manifestations of the fact that, for all our proud boasts that we live in an era of rationality, we do nothing of the sort.

We marriage counselors have tried to do something about this. We have developed the concept of marriage preparation. Drawing on our knowledge of the factors that cause marriages to fail, and tracing those factors back to their origins, we have discovered that many of them could have been eliminated if the couple had been helped, early in their association, to recognize the dangers and take appropriate steps to avoid them. If we are able by careful planning to anticipate and eliminate the awesome hazards involved in a voyage to the moon, it should not be beyond our power to steer most people around the hazards of matrimony. So we have reasoned, and offered our services.

These services, alas, have been largely spurned. The community is preoccupied with the plight of married couples already in serious trouble; and we have had to expend most of our efforts in the costly attempt to help them, despite the fact that the next group of marital breakdowns is already in process of being prepared for subsequent disaster and that preventing such future disaster would yield immensely greater rewards for a similar output of effort. All well-qualified marriage counselors would rather spend time with couples thinking about marriage, for whom they can often do a great deal, than with the desperate victims of marital shipwreck whose shrill cries for help assail their ears. But it is these latter who continually demand services and consume time, while the others go unheeding on their way, only to seek help years later when they in turn have made havoc of their marriages.

I have written this book in order to raise my voice in a plea that we should end this foolishness. My purpose is not, however, simply to cry in protest. What I prefer to do is to offer a plan, a proposal, that may provide something better. Let me outline it. It consists of a series of interviews between the engaged couple and an experienced professional person who is qualified to provide knowledge, to foster self-awareness, and to undertake counseling as it is required. I firmly and unhesitatingly affirm this to be the best way.

However, the situation we face is that large numbers of people—and their parents—have only the dimmest comprehension of all this, and therefore they are quite poorly motivated to see the service that could make a significant difference in their chances of marital success. My plan is to meet this difficulty by putting as much as possible of the marriage preparation process into the form of a book, and urging parents and friends to put it into the hands of engaged couples as a token of their goodwill. Once this is done, my hope is, naturally, that the couple will then read the book.

What I have done in these pages is to offer my readers, as far as is possible, exactly the program of marriage preparation which I would go through with them if they came to see me professionally. They can thus involve themselves in the process of looking at themselves and at each other that I would try to facilitate if I were working with them directly. If they undertake at all seriously the simple assignments I have set them, they will soon be seeing their relationship more realistically and communicating with each other at a deeper level.

Some couples need no more than this. If they encounter no serious problems as they do their "homework" together, they will have the satisfaction of knowing that they have met the tests and are ready for marriage. They will be in the position of couples whom the counselor dismisses with a blessing, and with every confidence that they are facing their future marriage realistically and have both the will and the wit to succeed in it.

We are then left with those who need direct help about problems which they simply will not be able to resolve by themselves. No book can do for them what is necessary, yet a book may bring home to them the fact that they must seek counseling help, and that it makes sense to do so. At that point, I have constituted myself a referral service. At various points within the book, I have indicated to couples who, in terms of their own resources, find themselves at the end of the road, that the time has now come to get direct help from a professional person. In Appendix 1, I have tried, carefully and in detail, to guide them in the task of finding a counselor who can give them the service they need. My hope is that, through reading the book and coming to understand how one marriage counselor works, they may feel comfortable enough about the process to overcome their natural hesitation and make that vital appointment which may mark a turning point in their lives.

I hope I have made my purpose entirely clear. This is not just a book *about* marriage or even about marriage preparation. It is an attempt to reach couples directly and through the enlightened cooperation of parents and friends who wish them well, and to present to them earnestly the case for adequate marriage preparation. It is also an attempt actually to involve them in the process of marriage preparation as far as this can possibly be done through the written word, and to show those for whom this means is not adequate how they can find their way to the most competent help available to them.

However, since I wrote the first edition of the book, I have come to see very clearly that even the best possible program of preparation for marriage may not be enough in itself, but that it should be followed up by guiding the couple through their critical first year together. I have dealt with this issue in chapter 13, which did not appear in the earlier edition of the book. I view this as being of the greatest importance. Experimental programs to help newlyweds work together for marital growth are now being developed, and they are proving to be highly successful.

My hope, therefore, is that I have been able to convey in the pages of this book my heartfelt wish for the couples who read it: that they may find through it the means to achieve in their marriages in the years ahead all the happiness and fulfillment that I have found in my marriage. I know of nothing better in human life that I could wish for them.

DAVID R. MACE

Part
One

Preparation

Why It Is So Important

The Purpose of This Book

*F*or every two couples in the United States who are at this moment on their way to getting married, one of them, at some future time, will end up getting divorced.

But for those who stay together, not all will be happy. Happiness in marriage is not an easy thing to measure. But estimates by well-informed people suggest that couples who don't break up often fall far below their potential for loving, rewarding relationships. Many of them, although they stay together, are secretly disillusioned. Indeed, as the years pass, the tendency is not for a couple to find more satisfaction in their marriage relationship, but rather to become increasingly dissatisfied. The trend of marital satisfaction may well go down, not up, throughout the life of the average marriage.

Is this a terrible way to start a book for people who are planning to marry? No, it isn't. These are facts, and they ought to be known and faced.

If you were planning a trip to Africa and consulted me about it because I happen to know Africa, I would be letting you down if I didn't tell you anything about the hazards and discomforts you would encounter. Just because there are hazards, however, I wouldn't advise you not to go to Africa. I would make my knowledge available to you by telling you how to avoid the hazards. I would try to plan with you a pleasant, rewarding, trouble-free trip.

This is exactly what I want to do in helping you to prepare for your marriage. I have now been a marriage counselor for some forty-five years. I helped to get marriage counseling started in England and in several other parts of the world and played a leading part in developing it professionally in the United States. During those years I have sat down for long hours with many couples in distress. I therefore know the hazards well, and there are plenty of them. But I am not discouraged about marriage on that account. On the contrary, I believe in it as much as, if not more than, I ever did. At its best it is a magnificent institution offering people tremendous rewards. Despite the difficulties, we know that married people in general are happier than single people, that they live longer, and that they enjoy better physical and mental health. These also are facts, and I can add to them the testimony of my own personal experience. The best thing I ever did in my life was to get married. Marriage has brought me more happiness than all the other pleasant experiences of my life combined.

Why then do so many people run into trouble? There are many reasons, and I will try to give you some of them later. But I will give you the main reason now. It is because people don't get the help they need about marriage either before they begin or after they get started. My experience as a counselor has brought me in touch with a great many married couples in trouble, and as I think of them two feelings sweep over me—compassion and anger. I feel compassion because these people, nearly all of them, wanted very much to achieve a warm, loving, mutually satisfying relationship. Yet they couldn't find what they sought, because they didn't understand the complexity of the task. They were ignorant, confused, bewildered. And when I think of their ignorance, then I begin to feel anger—anger with the smug, complacent indifference that prevents us from providing real help and guidance to most married people and to those moving into marriage. If all my long years as a marriage counselor have taught me anything, it is that the unhappy marriages in our midst represent a tragic and inexcusable waste of the best human resource we have—the capacity for love and trust and tenderness and comradeship and mutual support that most men and women have within them and that they deeply desire to develop in marriage for their happiness and fulfillment.

Albert Einstein is reported to have said that the average person, throughout life, uses only about 10 percent of his or her mental powers. The remaining 90 percent is wasted because it is never developed. Something like that, I believe, happens also in marriage. Large numbers of people have dreamed their dreams about the deep happiness a man and a woman can find in each other and can shape into the rich experience of a shared life. But the fulfillment of the dream has eluded them, and as they have gone through life they have become bitter, restless, and dissatisfied. They had the potential to realize a shared life of lasting love, but they never managed to realize it.

In today's world there is plenty of cynicism about marriage. This, of course, is nothing new. Marriage has always been a favorite theme for the wisecracks of the entertainers. Cynicism has at its root a pang of wistfulness, and a cynic's destructiveness springs from concealed hurt. A cynic is a disappointed, disillusioned person who has found life sour.

For that reason, the cynic is not a reliable guide to the state of marriage in our world today. Marriage has not been exposed as a fraud. It is not in a state of decline. Here is what Dr. Paul Glick, one of our foremost authorities on the subject, says of it, "The more I study the subject, the more apparent it becomes; marriage is regarded as the happiest, healthiest and most desired state of human existence. We get divorced not because we don't like marriage, but to find a better marriage partner. We live longer and are healthier if we are married. More of us are getting married, more of us are staying married longer." Marriage, in short, is still viewed as a happy, rewarding experience to which most people earnestly aspire. It is a misfortune that many fail to realize this hope. I believe, however, that it is a misfortune that can be remedied. Many, many more people could enjoy the blessing of a truly happy marriage, if only . . .

If only . . . What we need to do is to see marriage as a task, as a goal that is certainly difficult to attain but not unattainable. If we drift into marriage, thinking of it as a free gift handed to us on a silver platter by a smiling providence and guaranteed of itself to bring us lasting bliss, we are being utterly unrealistic. "We are in love, and that will take care of everything" is a very dangerous philosophy for any couple. Marriage is demanding. It calls for intelligence and effort and maturity and patience to achieve the rewards it has to offer. Sometimes, also, it requires outside help, the guidance and support of a skilled counselor.

In this book I am going to act as your premarital counselor. Of course it can't be a real counseling situation, because that requires face-to-face meetings and two-way communication. However, if you agree, we shall do as much as we can to set up the conditions of a series of marriage preparation interviews. I suggest that we do this in three ways:

1. I will talk over with you the areas I would try to cover if you (I am thinking of two of you, a thinking-of-getting-married couple) had in fact come to me for marriage preparation as hundreds of couples have come to me through the years. I will raise with you the questions about yourselves, your relationship, your hopes and fears, your plans and expectations that I would talk over with you if we were actually meeting together.

2. You can't talk back to me, but you can talk with each other. And this is what I would want you to do. Either you could read each section of the book together, stopping as you go along and discussing whatever seems to apply to your particular personal lives, or you could each read a section separately in advance, recording anything you ought to talk over with each other—either by underlining it in the book or by making notes on a separate sheet of

paper. Your discussion should take place in a leisurely setting, if possible in a secluded place where you are not likely to be interrupted.

3. If you become aware of areas in which you need help, you should find someone whom you both respect and trust to act as your counselor. I have prepared a special appendix to this book to help you to find a competent counselor. It could be a pastor, a marriage counselor, or some other professional person qualified to give you the kind of help you want. In some special areas you might get most help from a physician, a lawyer, or a financial counselor. There might be some questions that could best be talked over—separately or together—with a trusted friend in your own peer group or a married couple in whom you have confidence.

There are other ways in which the book might be used. Your pastor or a marriage counselor may have given you a copy as a means of helping you to identify and focus on the areas of your relationship where you might need help.

Another possibility I would strongly recommend is that you might get into a marriage preparation group. For some years now we have realized the great help a group of couples can give to one another. They are traveling together over the same stretch of the same road, and this gives them a great deal in common. If any such program is being offered in your community, I would urge you to join it. And if you can find nothing of the kind, you might even get together a group yourselves, or with the help of your pastor. The group could then agree to read certain sections of this book in preparation for each of its weekly meetings. Couples thinking about marriage and recently married couples mix well for this purpose, and one advantage is that the married couples can invite the group to meet in turn in their homes.

What I am trying to emphasize is that *the purpose of this book is to do something very practical*—with you and for you. For this reason, I will write very much in the way I would talk, avoiding all involved and technical language, and all speculative and theoretical ideas. We will try to stick to the facts—and to the down-to-earth facts that are important to you, a couple moving toward marriage. So, we are ready to begin.

compass, the other has neither. Which one is likely to find the way through?

You may say, of course, that marriage is not unknown territory. We see marriages all around us, and we know what the functions of husbands and wives are. But in fact we don't see marriages. All we see is the façade the couples present to the world. What goes on between them in the intimate life they share is hidden. One of the things most couples don't generally do in our culture is to talk about what goes on in their relationship, and especially about anything that disturbs them. Their every instinct is to conceal their conflicts and turn a brave and smiling face to the world. You know how often, when a marriage breaks up, friends and even relatives will exclaim, "This is so unexpected. We thought they were getting along fine."

The evidence is overwhelming that most couples go into marriage with quite inadequate understanding of the roles of husband and wife. Marriage counselors never cease to be amazed at the ignorance about marriage which they find in people otherwise well informed. There are at least two explanations of this. The first is that there is no clearly agreed time in life—at home, in school, in church, or anywhere else—when we give young people careful teaching about marriage. The second is that there is a persistent idea around that no special knowledge is needed in order to live together as a married couple. "It comes natural," people say. This is a serious illusion. The life of marriage is very complex, very demanding; the number of those who fail should be enough to make that clear. The sooner we face this undeniable fact the better.

So the prepared couple will have a great advantage over the couples who have not made themselves ready. They will understand what marriage involves, what adjustments have to be made. More important, they will have taken a good look both at themselves and at each other as persons, and they will know what they have to work with. They will understand the roles they have to play.

As I wrote some years ago in a foreword to Dr. Henry Bowman's excellent book *Marriage for Moderns*, "It is ridiculous to say, or to imply, that those who have learned something of the art of achieving a good marriage relationship will be no better off than those who know nothing about it."

2. *You will be able to make the critical early adjustments of marriage smoothly and quickly.* Auto mechanics tell us that the way a car is treated in the first thousand miles will have a deep and lasting influence on the way it behaves later. Something like that is true also of the marriage relationship. We now know that the shape of a marriage develops quite early. In the first six or twelve months a couple develop habits of behaving toward each other that become settled and are not easily changed later. These habits decide a number of important questions: who plays the dominant and who the submissive role, who takes major responsibility for the different areas of the couple's shared life, how quarrels are handled, who initiates the first move to make up, who makes the final decisions in what areas, how household chores are allocated, how money is managed, how sexual needs are met, relationships with in-laws or former friends or neighbors, how leisure time is spent. These are just a few of the many areas in which patterns are developed in the early months of marriage. We shall discuss most of them in more detail later.

It is obvious that the way in which these patterns develop will have a great influence on the future of the marriage. Develop a set of good patterns, and the marriage will be off to a promising start. Drift into unsatisfactory and destructive ways of interacting in these areas, and the seeds are sown that will lead to all kinds of later trouble and conflict.

The unprepared, who have not thought about these matters, will allow patterns to develop in an unplanned, haphazard fashion. The prepared will try to do better. I am not suggesting, of course, that you can make an intellectual decision about how you will live together, and then just go ahead and carry it out. We are influenced in the way we behave by the habits of a lifetime, and by the time we reach the age of marriage we can change ourselves only to a limited extent. Nevertheless, I have been convinced by my experience as a marriage counselor that a genuine willingness on the part of husband and wife to understand each other, to recognize the need for change, and to make sincere attempts to change as far as possible, can in most cases result in a very satisfying degree of mutual adaptation. I am also convinced that it is much easier to do this in the early months of marriage than to try to do it later when habit patterns have become set, and when the motivation to make changes has run down.

3. *You will have a better chance of reaching higher levels of marital fulfillment.* Human relationships, as we are coming to understand them today, are very complex mechanisms. A marriage is perhaps the most complex of all because husband and wife live in the closest and most intimate of all adult relationships, and they play a great many roles and interact at a great many different levels.

What this means is that the *potential* in a marriage is likely to be greater than the couple ever realize. They can settle for any one of a wide range of levels. Some married couples live very superficially together. They communicate about routine matters, but do not share their deepest thoughts. They live almost separate lives under one roof. They meet each other's elementary needs but never venture into what I call relationship-in-depth. Surprisingly enough, they may never even really get to know each other, because all they reveal is a limited area of their true selves. They simply live together on the basis of a mutual exchange of services. He "brings home the bacon," she takes care of the house, she gives him sex, he gives her children. Based on a few such elementary exchanges, the marriage soon becomes dull and dreary.

Such mediocre marriages are still very common in our culture. Yet often these very people are tormented by the longing for a relationship that is richer, deeper, and more meaningful. They are love-starved, and often they turn in other directions to seek what marriage has failed to give them. The wife may become almost completely preoccupied with her children, the husband gets immersed in his job, either or both may turn to extramarital affairs in the effort to find more satisfying love experiences.

Any couple who choose in marriage to develop their full potential and to seek relationship-in-depth will need to prepare and to work hard in the early years of their life together. For the making of a really good marriage is seldom brought about by chance. Like any other work of art, it is the result of informed, purposeful striving and creative effort.

4. *You will increase your chances of being successful parents.* Nowadays, many people fail to realize seriously the qualitative relationship between marriage and parenthood. The two are very intimately bound up together.

Physically, it is easy for any man and woman to bring about the conception of a child. They do not even have to know each other, let alone have a significant relationship. But once the child is conceived, the woman can adjust to pregnancy much better if she is sustained and supported by her child's other parent. And the child who is born needs increasingly the support and guidance both of a mother and a father.

All this we know well. It is one of the major purposes of marriage. But what we fail to stress is that as the child grows up, his or her need is not simply for two parents, but for *two parents who love each other* and love the child as an expression and extension of their love for each other. It is their mutual affection that creates the atmosphere that gives the child emotional security. Their united faith in their child shapes that child's sense of purpose for his or her own life.

Of all the gifts which parents can offer to a child of their love, therefore, the greatest is that of a happy marriage. For this guarantees that the child will be surrounded by the united love of both the child's parents. In their pattern of discipline they will support each other, so that the child's world will be one of coherent order. Their goal for the child will be fully shared. And because they find their love needs richly fulfilled in each other, they will be able to bestow a love that makes no adult demands which he or she cannot meet. Because they are not in conflict, the child will not be inwardly torn by the need to struggle with a divided loyalty.

I once wrote an article with the title, "Be Happily Married—For Your Children's Sake." My plea was that even if a married couple won't make the effort to work at their marriage for the rewards it can bring *them,* they should consider doing so for the rewards it can enable them to offer their children. This would apply equally to preparation for marriage. If you don't feel inclined to make the effort for the sake of your own future happiness, then make it for the happiness of your children yet unborn.

5. *You will understand the wisdom of seeking marriage counseling in good time if you ever come to need it.* One of the exasperations of the marriage counselor is that people often delay coming for help until it is too late for much to be done. By the time they come, they have built up attitudes of hostility and resentment that have almost destroyed their love and poisoned their relationship. Sometimes, they have already found ways of escape from each other and have developed new love relationships outside of marriage. To help such people is difficult, and it means sometimes an impossible task.

People who have sought preparation for marriage have more sense. They are less likely, of course, to get into trouble. But if they do encounter serious conflict that they can't resolve by their own unaided efforts, they know what this means. They realize that there is no time to be lost, that they must get help before the destructive process of degeneration sets in and they begin to be progressively alienated from each other. They are enlightened enough to realize that marital health, like physical and mental health, must be closely watched, and professional help sought as soon as there are signs of possible serious trouble.

An even better plan is to provide programs to follow up marriage preparation by guiding the couple through their first year together. I shall return to this issue later in the book.

Summary

I hope I have convinced you that a strong case can be made for marriage preparation. Not only your own happiness as a couple, but also the happiness of your children, and quite possibly of other people as well, may depend upon it. Those who have prepared for marriage increase their chances of avoiding needless misery, of moving more quickly into the rich fulfillment that marriage has to offer, and of reaching a deeper quality of relationship than they might otherwise be able to achieve.

It makes sense, doesn't it?

3

Marriage as It Is Today

$\mathcal{B}$efore we begin to talk about you as a particular and very special couple, we ought to be sure that we understand marriage in our contemporary world—what it demands, what it offers, and how different it is from marriage in the past.

Outwardly, marriage seems to be the same now as it always was. Two people, a man and a woman, come together and enter into a shared life. Together they create a new unit of human society. They set up a home, children are born to them, and they establish what we call a family. Husband and wife have their own special tasks, but they cooperate to help and support each other, and they work together to raise their children as useful members of the community. In due course, their children reach the age at which they are ready to marry, and the cycle of life goes on into another generation. Marriage is the foundation stone of the family, just as the family is the foundation stone of the community.

This has been the way in which most human beings have lived their lives for as far back as we can trace human societies throughout the world. The details have varied—in some cultures a man has been allowed more than one wife at a time, occasionally a woman has had more than one husband. But the broad pattern has never been changed.

Some people today talk about the family as an outworn

institution, and even say that yours may be the last generation that will accept marriage. These are statements that are not supported by the facts. We have no convincing evidence that marriage and family life will not continue in the future as they have continued since human life began; if only because there is no other way we know of to provide satisfactorily for the needs men and women meet in each other, and for the all-important task of passing on to children what they require in order to take over the task of safeguarding our human values and maintaining our human culture. Many experiments have been made throughout human history to find alternatives to marriage and family life. None of them has endured for long.

However, if marriage is not in danger of extinction, it is certainly undergoing some profound changes which need to be clearly understood by every modern couple. The changes in marriage simply reflect the changes in our society, as we move from a rural-agricultural to an urban-industrial way of life. It isn't only marriage that is changing today, everything is changing. Conservative older people find this very disturbing. They want to sit still where they have always sat; but to their annoyance, they find themselves carried along on a vast conveyor belt, traveling to an unknown future. This not only annoys them, it alarms them. The mood of such people was well expressed by the title of a play that ran some years ago on Broadway, *Stop the World, I Want to Get Off*.

Change, however, need not be threatening. On the whole, our human lot today is better than it has ever been throughout our long history. At least the means to enjoy "the good life" are ours as never before; what we do about it depends on ourselves. This is equally true of marriage. It is possible for more people today to have better marriages than people have ever had at any previous time. The changes, when they are properly understood, are favorable to marriage at its best.

The heart of the change is summed up in the subtitle of a book written by one of the most distinguished sociologists who has studied the family in this century, Dr. Ernest W. Burgess. The phrase he used to describe the trend in marriage was "From Institution to Companionship."

We can clearly see the changes now taking place in three significant areas of marriage.

The Founding of a Marriage

In the past, marriage was first and foremost a social obligation. Setting up families and having children were essential to the survival of the tribe or community. So marriages were planned and arranged by the elders; or at least, the approval of the elders was needed before the couple were allowed to marry. When married, they usually lived with the husband's parents, or at least nearby on the family land. They were supervised and guided by their in-laws, because they would ultimately take on the task of caring for the family property, maintaining the family traditions, and continuing the family name and line through their children. So the ideal was that a boy married a girl from a neighboring farm, who had been educated in the same school, had attended the same church, and whose parents shared the same political opinions as his own parents.

Nowadays, this has changed. People choose their own marriage partners and parents have very little say in the choice. People often meet their future husbands and wives away from their home community, in college or at work in another city. Husband and wife may come from different religions, from different ethnic backgrounds, from different races. One may have been raised in the country, the other in the city. One may come from a poor home, while the family of the other may be comparatively wealthy. They may hold very different views on many subjects and even have very different values and standards.

When modern people marry, they are not likely to settle near their parents. Often they start out alone in a community where both are a long way from home. They do have the telephone to enable them to keep in touch, and visits back to the home community are easier to make nowadays. But most of their time will be spent with friends and neighbors whose customs and traditions are likely to be very different from those of their childhood homes. And perhaps they won't stay long with those new friends and neighbors. American families move a great deal—on the average, one in five changes its home every year. In some communities, the rate of mobility is higher even than this.

Clearly these new circumstances make marriage more difficult in a number of ways. Differences in customary ways of running the home, spending the money, fulfilling the roles of husband and wife, father and mother, will cause confusion, and major adjustments will be needed before the couple can settle down happily together. "That wasn't the way I was taught to act" will become a familiar phrase, and each time it is said there will be a real possibility of conflict. Far more adjustments are needed to enable a marriage of this kind to succeed than are needed for a couple who begin with a common cultural background. This is abundantly demonstrated by the fact that sociological studies have discovered again and again that the most stable marriages are those between partners who have come from the same or similar communities. Other things being equal, the more diversity there is in cultural, religious, and racial backgrounds, the tougher is the task of overcoming the difficulties and making the marriage work.

The Marriage Partnership

We have been speaking of marriage in relation to its social environment. But when we look into the relationship between husband and wife, here also there have been tremendous changes.

In human history it seems that marriage has often produced undesirable conflict. In the older cultures,

disturbances were avoided by two special devices. One
was to decide in advance which of the two would be boss.
Needless to say, it was always the husband! In the Orient,
the duty of the wife was made perfectly clear; she must
obey her husband in all matters. He made the major
decisions; she accepted them. So there was no clash of
conflicting wills, and peace reigned in the home. It was the
woman, of course, who paid the price.

The other way of avoiding conflict was to separate the
duties of husband and wife so that they didn't come into
collision with each other. Generally speaking, the wife's
sphere was in the home. The husband was responsible for
the outside work, together with a few jobs in the house
that required greater physical strength or mechanical skill.
So they had their separate spheres of influence and didn't
interfere unduly with each other.

Today all this is changed. Women have been emancipated. Today's couple think of marriage as an equal
partnership in which both share. Decisions are no longer
made on a one-vote system; both partners have equal
votes. The line between man's work and woman's work
still exists, but it is becoming less and less clear. The wife
of today who holds a responsible job outside the home
and may bring home a paycheck that is equal to or greater
than that of her husband is simply not prepared to be a
meek little mouse, doing what she is told and subjecting
her will to her husband's pleasure.

All this results in far more confusion and conflict than
were likely in the marriage of the past. A two-vote system
is much harder to operate than a one-vote system. Again
and again the votes may be equally split. Then the issue
must be decided by negotiation, which can be a
long-drawn-out and complicated process. If the wife puts
in an eight-hour day outside the home, it is hardly fair to
expect her in addition to deal with all the household
chores. So, because the modern wife is emancipated, the
modern husband must be domesticated.

In today's marriages there are fewer and fewer
stereotyped patterns. The roles of husband and wife have

to be decided to meet their particular personal situation. As Dr. Joseph Folsom once put it, the first thing the modern married couple need to do is to draw up a constitution for their life together, to decide who does what, when, and how. This makes much greater demands on both, and in consequence it is much easier for the marriage to become deadlocked.

Of course, marriage that is a truly equal partnership between husband and wife can be very rewarding. It provides a relationship in which each can freely contribute his or her gifts to the common welfare, and so develop a deep and satisfying comradeship. The modern marriage, therefore, offers greater possibilities of mutual satisfaction, but at a far higher price than before. It is not really surprising that many become disillusioned and give up the attempt.

The Task of Parenthood

The primary function of marriage has always been to produce children. In many cultures, a childless marriage is simply dissolved; it has failed to work. "Be fruitful and multiply" is the best-known injunction the Bible gives to married people. And in the past it has been necessary to have many children in order to preserve the family and tribe. In some parts of the world even today, as many as half of all children born die in their first year of life, and many who survive die before reaching maturity. So, the people argue, you must have many children to be sure of raising a few who can take over the family's duties and look after their aging parents.

Now this also has changed completely. Having many children today doesn't ensure our survival. If all couples had large families, we are told, we would soon be facing disaster. So the small family is the order of the day. In some ways, this certainly makes less work. But in other ways, it puts new responsibilities on the shoulders of the parents. In big families, older children took care of the younger, and often they solved each other's problems. Now each child needs a great deal of special individual care from the parents. The child needs, too, a long and expensive education before he or she is ready to be a responsible adult. And the child grows up in a pluralistic society and may challenge what the parents have taught and may even rebel against them.

Modern patterns of child-raising, therefore, have to be different. In the old days, the aim was to produce obedient children who would accept their parents' authority, believe everything they said, and do what they were told. "Little children," it was often said, "should be seen and not heard." They were not expected to have opinions of their own; and even when they did have opinions they were not encouraged to express them. Under these conditions, the task of parenthood was fairly manageable.

That kind of parenthood doesn't work anymore. Modern children grow up in an open society where they enjoy a degree of personal freedom quite unknown in the past. Obeying elders won't get them very far, because the elders disagree about what is good and right. For today's parents, the task of child-raising is to cooperate with the children and teach them to make wise decisions, to use freedom with responsibility. This is a far more complex task and requires of parents that they be enlightened, mature, infinitely patient, and above all united. This in turn makes great demands on marriage. Large numbers of married couples today are burdened with an oppressive sense of having failed as parents and are weary and heartsick about it. There is no evidence as yet that parenthood is getting any easier.

Summary

What this all adds up to is the fact that marriage today is no longer the comparatively easy process of following a standard blueprint. Each individual marriage has a character of its own and presents the couple with a disconcerting array of difficult tasks to be performed if the goal of a happy and harmonious family life is to be achieved. Yet at the same time, marriage today has much to offer in terms of individual fulfillment and personality development and in emotional security, which the more rigid and stable marriages of the past often failed to make possible. There have, of course, been very happy marriages at all periods of our human history. Yet I would repeat that the chances of achieving very high levels of fulfillment are better today, for more people, than ever before.

The rewards are great, but the task is difficult. The moral is, be prepared.

Part
Two

Yourselves

What You Bring to Each Other

4

How Well Do You Know Yourself?

*L*et me explain what we are going to do in this section of the book. First, I am going to ask each of you to look at yourself—who you are, how you came to be what you are, where you stand now, and what you are asking of life. Second, I shall invite you both to share with each other, as far as you feel able, what you have come to know and understand about yourselves. Third, I shall suggest that you discuss what it might mean to you as a couple to spend the rest of your lives together in the most intimate, and the most demanding, of all human relationships.

These are exactly the steps I would want you to take if you were coming to me for marriage preparation interviews. I would spend at least one hour with each of you separately, going over what we call your personal history. As you responded, I would make notes. After I had seen each of you separately, I would make an appointment for both of you to come together. Before I met with you, I would sit down with my notes and think about you, trying to picture you married to each other. I would consider what were the strengths in your relationship, the areas in which you would be in agreement, in which you would naturally support and fortify each other. Then I would consider the areas in which you would probably disagree or find yourselves in conflict (there are always some of these, even in the very well-matched couples).

When we sat down all together, I would encourage you yourselves to try to identify your strong points and your likely conflict areas, and I would check your impressions against my own. I could easily find that my estimates were wrong and had to be modified. After all, I would only have spent about an hour with each of you. But I might find, also, that I had spotted some things in your relationship that you had been unaware of, or at least things you had preferred not to think about or to face up to. We would talk together about all these matters during one or more interviews, taking whatever time proved to be necessary.

Let me make my aim very clear. I want you to come out of this experience with as clear a picture as you can obtain of yourselves as a couple. Why? Because it is far better to come to terms with the realities now than to be rudely awakened to them later. One reason for this is that you obviously would feel cheated later if you discovered important things about each other that you should have known before. Such an experience can produce bitterness and resentment, and feelings of that kind don't provide the right atmosphere for the adjustments that then have to be made.

The other reason for getting a clear picture of each other before marriage is that a great many of the adjustments you will have to make can begin during the premarriage period. In fact, one of the most worthwhile uses you can make of the months before your marriage is to get to know each other really well. Not all the serious conflicts you may have to face in marriage will necessarily emerge before you become husband and wife, yet it is probable that you will become vaguely aware of most of them at one time or another in the early period of your acquaintance. As a couple looking toward marriage you can do a great deal of growing together, and this is in fact the best possible way of preparing for your future.

Many people think of marriage preparation as learning about marriage now so as to be able, when the time comes, to handle the various adjustments that will have to be made later to sex, to money, to in-laws, and so on. It is quite true that knowledge about these matters will be valuable to you, and ideally every couple should have such knowledge. However, the real purpose of this knowledge is not to tuck it away at the back of your mind for future use, but to make use of it now. Already you are coping, at least in a preliminary way, with most of the issues that will come up in full force when you become husband and wife. You are already dealing with sex, money, and in-laws; and the way you manage them now will provide guidelines for handling them later.

In other words, marriage is not going to change the relationship that is already developing between you, but will only intensify it by enabling it to be more intimate, more continuous, and more demanding. So the best way in which you can prepare for your future marriage is to learn to be, here and now, a really sucessfully functioning couple. Your present, if it is well and wisely handled, will in many respects decide your future. Every successful adjustment you make to each other now will be a credit that you can carry over into the next stages of your growth as a couple.

I am well aware that this idea of working on your relationship now may raise problems for you. One is a reaction I have often encountered. As one woman put it, "This is a very special time in our lives, which we want to enjoy to the full. Looking at ourselves in the way you suggest is like questioning our love for each other. I'm afraid it might spoil the romance."

I understand this anxiety. But the argument simply doesn't stand up. If you are just dating for fun, you don't need to get to know each other in depth. But when you are thinking seriously of marrying you simply have to face the facts, and it is quite irresponsible to refuse to do so. As to the argument that it would spoil your romance, that depends entirely on what you mean to each other. If you are still at the stage of projecting on each other your adolescent dreams of fairy princes and princesses, I have to tell you plainly as your counselor, even at the risk of offending you, that it is now time to wake up, to exchange the land of dreams for the world of reality.

Your love for each other must be tested at this time. And if you truly love each other, knowing each other better will strengthen that love, not weaken it. As a matter of fact, one of the results of love between a man and a woman is a tremendous interest in each other that makes them want to know each other better and better. If you don't have this urge, perhaps you need to ask yourself whether after all you are only "in love with love."

Another problem I may have raised for you was expressed in this way by John: "I frankly don't like this idea of telling Peg all about myself. There are some things I would rather keep to myself. She isn't the first girl I have gone around with, you know. And if I told her some of the things that happened with the others, we might break up. I am not prepared to risk that."

What should people do about confessions? This boy naturally wanted to make the best possible impression on the girl he hoped to marry. That is what we all do during courtship, just as the male bird spreads his feathers before the female to show her what a fine fellow he is. However, as courtship leads on to marriage, the truth is that you can't successfully conceal your real self from the one you love, and it becomes more and more of a strain to try to do so.

In marriage we have to accept each other as we are. The failure to do this only leads to trouble. So if John is trying to hide from Peg something of himself which she will discover sooner or later, it's best to let her know now and take the consequences. People should go into marriage knowing all the really relevant facts about each other. If you can't begin your life together in honesty, the chances that you will ever develop a deep trust in each other are pretty poor.

However, this doesn't mean that John has to report to Peg in detail all the things he did, sexually and otherwise, with his previous girl friends. This might be quite an upsetting experience for Peg, and she would probably prefer not to hear such details.

I offer you a simple rule about confessions. If you feel you must make them, and you are quite sure you can do so in a loving way that won't cause distress to your partner, go ahead. But if you are in doubt about it, follow this plan. Go first and make the confession in full to someone you respect and trust, and discuss whether it would be good to make the confession to the one you plan to marry. If the decision on which you both agree is not to do so, you should find that the matter won't worry you any further. You have shown your willingness to tell, and that is what matters most. If at some later time the facts should come out, and your marriage partner asks you why you didn't confess before, your reply is that you were quite willing to do so, and that you *have* in fact told someone (whom you could name). You then explain that you withheld the confession from your partner, because it seemed at the time to be the most loving thing to do.

Now we should be ready to begin, if you are willing. We will start with each of you separately. Since I can't be actually present with you to take notes, I suggest that you get a pencil and paper and put down, as we look at your personal history, whatever you think is important. Then you can each go over your notes carefully, take a good look at yourself, and decide how to present the results of your individual thinking to the other.

There is another way to do this, and you may prefer it. Let me tell you how one couple went about it. There was a parking place on a hill, from which they could gain a commanding view of the city where they lived. On a succession of evenings, they drove to this spot. They took turns telling their life stories to each other, just everything about their earlier lives they could think of. They finally reached a point at which each was able to say to the other, "Now I'm through. You know as much about me as I know about myself." According to their testimony, they found the experience a very rewarding one.

The method doesn't matter. What does matter is that any two people who plan to spend their whole lives together ought to know each other pretty well at the start. If there is any time in life at which you could with profit take a long, hard look at yourself, surely it is just before you entrust your life and happiness to another.

5

What Made You What You Are?

$\mathcal{T}$he traditional challenge of the sentry is, "Halt! Who goes there?" Before being allowed to pass, you must identify yourself. So it should be with marriage. Before being allowed in, you should identify yourself to yourself and to your partner.

But how do you identify yourself? It can be done at two very different levels. The first is to describe yourself on the outside in terms of labels: age, education, job, religion, politics, and so on. But that doesn't identify the real you, the kind of person you are, any more than your photograph does. Despite the movie caricatures, in real life it is impossible to tell heroes from villains by their looks. If I listed your general description in terms of the labels you wear and published it with the offer of ten thousand dollars if this person would come forward, I would probably have quite a number of applicants to deal with. There would be honest and dishonest people, generous and mean people, responsible and irresponsible people, all answering your general description.

The other way of identifying yourself is by association with another person, in which you open up your inner self and reveal the kind of person you really are. Of course, this is what is important in marriage. What matters is what you are like inside and how you are likely to relate to the person to whom you are closest in the world.

In this chapter, I am inviting you (each of you

separately) to take a good look at yourself. This is not an easy thing to do. Self-assessment can be unreliable, because you have built up defenses against recognizing some realities about yourself which you would rather not acknowledge. Many people don't accept themselves as they are; they try desperately to appear before the world as other than they are. They try to appear more honest, more educated, more handsome (with the aid of clothes and makeup), more pleasant (by concealing their ill temper). In fairly superficial relationships this pays off, and we all do it to some extent.

In the intimate life of marriage, however, this just isn't going to work. There our pretenses are stripped away, and we appear before each other as we really are. Therefore, since you are looking at yourself now as a prospect for marriage, it must be an honest look at the real you because that's the person your partner is going to live with.

The best way to know yourself as you are is to understand the forces that have shaped your personality. You didn't make yourself. You came into the world with certain basic endowments. But you became what you are now as a result of the way in which you reacted and adapted to the conditions under which you lived and to the people you had to get along with. So let us look now at these major influences in your life and what they have made of you.

For convenience, we shall divide up your personal history into nine aspects.

Your Family Background

This aspect is by far the most important, and we could spend a lot of time on it. Up to now, your parents have almost certainly been the most influential people in your life. Your basic endowment came either from them or through them from earlier ancestors. They shaped your life almost exclusively in your formative early years, and they have probably continued to have a deep and powerful influence over you. Most of your ways of behaving have been either copied from them consciously or unconsciously, or have developed out of your rebellion against them.

Look now, therefore, at your parents. What was your basic relationship to each of them? Were you close to both of them? To one, but not the other? To neither of them? By closeness, I mean warmly expressed love, affection, and trust. A good test is to ask how far you felt able to confide in them.

Closeness to parents is good in the childhood years. But if that closeness continued in your teen years so that it was difficult for you to free yourself and establish your independence, did the closeness become dominance on your parents' side? That is not so good.

Another question to ask is, how did they raise you? Were you satisfied with the way in which you were disciplined? Did you feel you were well understood? Did you feel you received fair treatment? In general, patterns of discipline that are too severe or too lax harm the child. What is best is a pattern that is firm but fair.

Try to evaluate, also, their relationship to each other. A child sees in his or her parents a close-up demonstration of the way in which a man and a woman relate to each other, and that deeply influences the child's own expectations. Parents are role models. A boy learns from his father how a man treats a woman, and from his mother how a woman responds to a man. A girl likewise learns from her parents how the masculine and feminine roles are played.

A good way to evaluate the influence of your parents is to ask yourself, "What things in the life of my parental home would I want to carry over into my own home? What things would I not want to carry over?"

If you decide that you were the happy child of warm, loving parents with whom you enjoyed a close and confiding relationship, by whom you were not hindered in your growth to independence, and whose pattern of married love you would want to repeat in your own marriage, you have reason to feel fortunate. This, according to research findings, doubles your chances of successful marriage. If you came from an unhappy home, however, that does not condemn you to marital misery. It simply alerts you to the fact that you may have to work a bit harder than the average person to ensure success.

Your Social Adjustment

You have developed your own individual methods of relating to other people, and these will certainly affect the way in which you relate to your marriage partner. So you should now try to understand your pattern of social adjustment.

As well as your parents, your brothers and sisters influenced you here. If you were an older child, you probably had to take some responsibility for the others. If you were the youngest in the family, you were probably indulged, though you may have been the one everyone picked on, too. If you were an only child, you probably felt important and got used to being in the center of the whole picture, yet outside the family you could have found relationships difficult. These are only some of the patterns that develop. Try to figure out what yours was.

Then look at your relationship to others outside the family. Did you have plenty of childhood friends, or were you lonely and withdrawn? How did you rank in the group of kids you played with? Did you take the lead? Or were you just one of the crowd, going along with what the others decided? Or did you feel inferior and inadequate?

As you grew up, how did you learn to react to other people in your life? Have you become confident and self-assured? Insecure and self-conscious? Or something in between? Do you react with apprehension or hostility when you meet new people for the first time? If so, do you express this openly, or try to conceal it behind a surface politeness? In your social circle, do you like a party atmosphere with plenty of people around? Or are you more at ease with a few trusted buddies? When you are upset and hurt, do you spill out your feelings or withdraw into yourself and avoid other people until you have recovered your composure?

It will be obvious to you that your answers to these and other similar questions will give you valuable clues about how you are likely to react to a very close and continuous relationship with a marriage partner. Try to assess your assets and liabilities in this important area.

Your Intellectual Development

How much formal education did you get? This will clearly determine to some extent the kind of people you like to talk with. A person much more ignorant than yourself would be apt to become boring. Someone who knew much more than you did could make you feel inferior.

Did you measure up, as a student, to what your parents and teachers expected of you and to what you expected of yourself? If not, do you suffer from feelings of intellectual inadequacy in relating to other people so that you avoid discussions of matters you don't understand and are afraid to admit ignorance in case people will think you stupid? If you know you are not a highly intelligent person, have you accepted this comfortably, recognizing that you have other good qualities that your friends can appreciate?

Your Vocational Development

Have you found the kind of work you can do well and take pride in? Or are you restlessly trying to prove yourself to yourself and to others? To be contented and confident in your job is vital to your self-esteem and happiness. It may be vital also to the happiness of your partner. A person driven relentlessly by unsatisfied ambitions can be very difficult to live with.

Are you satisfied that your vocational plans can assure

your family of economic security and provide you and
them with what will be needed to live in reasonable
comfort?

Your Spare-Time Interests

Given a stretch of time with no commitments and no
obligations, how would you choose to spend it? In other
words, to what kind of activities do you naturally turn
when all these outside pressures are off? The answer to
this question can tell you a good deal about the kind of
person you really are, about what makes you tick.

Do you tend, in such a situation, to seek the company of
others or to prefer seclusion? Are you motivated toward
hobbies that enable you to compete successfully and
prove your worth? Or to creative enterprises that give you
inward satisfaction? Or to escapist activities that enable
you to forget your anxieties and responsibilities?

Your Spiritual Development

What does religion mean to you? Is it a matter of
conforming to rules and customs you were brought up to
obey? Or is it a matter of group loyalty, feeling that you
belong to a company of people who give you a sense of
security and support? Or is your religion a deeply
personal source of strength and purpose in your life?

What is your basic philosophy of life? What are the
standards of personal integrity you try to meet? How
would you describe your fundamental goal in life? Is it
essentially a quest for personal satisfaction and fulfillment? Or would you call yourself "service-oriented"? Do
you consider that both can be combined?

How does this affect your sense of your duties and
obligations to others, especially those to whom you are
closely related? Do you tend to use them for your own
ends? How far can you find genuine satisfaction in making
others happy? How far can you tolerate faults in other

people and be patient and understanding toward them? Does your caring for your friends extend to sacrificing your own immediate goals if necessary in order to help them achieve their goals?

Your Sexual Experiences

Would you say that you feel basically comfortable about your own sexuality? Or is this an area of your life that creates anxiety, guilt, or insecurity?

In your past, were you helped to develop an essentially positive feeling about sex as something good and healthy? Or was it experienced as part of yourself that was dirty, disreputable, or unwholesome? Did you have sexual experiences—masturbation, homosexuality, seduction, casual sexual encounters—that left you feeling hurt and disturbed?

If you have had experiences of premarital sexual intercourse, of what kind have they been? Were you persuaded into them against your better judgment? Did you get into them with a divided mind? Have they left you with a guilty conscience? Did they involve exploitation of those with whom you shared them?

Your approach to marriage can be deeply affected by skeletons in the closet in this area. If you are troubled about this, it might be of great help to go and talk it all over with a marriage counselor.

Your Love Relationships

What have been your experiences of dating, of going steady, of falling in and out of love? Have they been pleasant and carefree, enabling you to grow and find yourself? Have you been able to function as a loving, caring person? Or have you had difficulties in this area?

Apart from sex, have you been able to enjoy experiences of intimacy with people you have loved? Have you learned to share your deepest feelings with such people, and to be open about yourself? Have you found that you could handle awkward situations, differences of opinion, conflicts about each other's attitudes and behavior, by talking things over honestly and so restoring the original mutual warmth and affection?

Have you had ugly, painful experiences in which you have been exploited or let down by people you loved and trusted? Have you yourself damaged your relationship with others by developing uncontrollable anger, frustration, hostility, or by finding yourself unable to cope with the tumult of your own feelings and having to break the relationship and escape from it?

Physical and Mental Health

What has been your health record? Have you had any serious illnesses or major accidents or operations? How have these affected you? Did they make you feel unable to achieve your goals? Did they cause you to be overprotected as a child? Do you have any disabilities that restrict you in any way from living a normal life or that would affect you as a marriage partner or as a parent?

What about your mental health? Have you suffered from any kind of nervous or emotional breakdown? Was it satisfactorily cleared up, or could it recur under conditions of stress?

How would you describe your temperament? Are you on the whole a contented, cheerful person? Or do you tend to be often gloomy and depressed? Do you experience wide changes of mood, from enthusiasm to despair? Are there situations in which you are overwhelmed with dread or panic? Is your basic attitude to life one of self-confidence or one of fear and apprehension?

Summary

I have raised a great many questions about you as a person and I could have raised a great many more. My suggestion is that you respond to these questions, and others that occur to you, by writing down your evaluation of yourself in these general areas. It is especially important to note any area that arouses anxiety or emotional tension in you and to try to discover why you are affected in this way. It will surely be clear to you why these aspects of your life may have a bearing on your future; the whole of what you are is going to be involved in the experience of sharing life totally with the one you love.

Your evaluation of yourself is your own. But I hope that you can share most of it with your future partner in a joint session. And if you find yourself confused or perplexed about any aspect of yourself that we have considered, it might save you a lot of unnecessary unhappiness, now and later, to get counseling help about it. Seeking help in understanding yourself is not a sign of weakness. It is a manifestation of wisdom and good judgment.

6

Where Are You Now?

I am assuming that you both have now taken a good look at yourselves, individually and separately, and have been able to follow this up by sharing your self-evaluations with each other. The next step is to look at yourselves, not separately but in combination, to make an evaluation of yourselves jointly as a couple moving toward marriage.

I should explain to you at this point that there are two distinct factors that influence success in marriage. One is the *marriageability* of each of the partners, the combination of qualities you individually possess that is favorable to good marital adjustment. It is at these qualities that we have been looking. But there is also another factor, perhaps of equal importance. This is your *compatibility*, how well you are suited, not to marriage generally, but to each other. We are now going to look at this, and it will be best for you to do it together.

The first obvious question to ask is, how did you two happen to move toward each other, to see in each other something good and attractive, and to develop your relationship to the point at which you now plan to marry?

You will never be able to answer that question fully, because it concerns a very complex process in which some deeply unconscious motivations in both of you have been at work. However, as far as it is possible to formulate your answer, you should try to do so.

Our Mate-Selection System

In the old days, as we have seen, mate selection was often arranged by the parents. Now people make their own choices. In order to adjust to this change, we have evolved in our Western world a system of mate selection which, on the whole, is very sound, provided you work it properly. You might like to compare your own experience with the general pattern.

The system works in three stages. First, there is *random dating*, an arrangement to allow boys and girls to learn to be comfortable with each other socially. A boy and a girl will go out together for a pleasant evening and enjoy each other's company without any commitment on either side. This enables young people in early adolescence to get over any self-consciousness they may have in the presence of the opposite sex, to learn to talk and feel at ease with each other, and to get some idea of the kind of partner they get along with most happily and comfortably. Dating is used for purposes other than this, but this is the major argument in favor of it, and it is a pretty convincing one.

The second stage is what used to be called *courtship*, a steady relationship between a boy and a girl who have found that they get along especially well with each other and are at this point more interested in getting to know each other better than in continued random dating. Often they will feel that they are in love, and they may talk at least tentatively about the possibility of marriage at some future time. But this stage involves no commitment. If, as they spend more time together, they seem after all not to be as well suited to each other as they at first thought, they will recognize this and break up. Parting may be temporarily a painful experience for one or for both, but recovery is usually quite rapid and complete.

If, however, the couple find, as they get to know each other better, that they do indeed have a great deal to give to each other, they may become more deeply involved in each other's lives; and if they feel they are old enough, they may now definitely decide to marry. This is the third stage, generally called *engagement*. Traditionally it has meant that the boy gives the girl a ring as an outward token that they are definitely planning to marry, and often a tentative date is now set for the wedding. This means a definite commitment on the part of both. But if, as time passes, they begin to have serious doubts about whether to go on to marriage, they can break the engagement—in fact, about one-third of all formal engagements today are broken. At this stage, a break may be quite painful and embarrassing, but it is far better to end an engagement when real doubts arise than to go on into a marriage that might end in disaster.

This mate-selection system is a good one—in fact, I cannot imagine anything better. Each stage can be a learning process. At each stage the quality of the relationship is tested, and at each stage it can be terminated if it fails to measure up to the test. Properly used, this system should give most people a good chance to find a compatible marriage partner. Unfortunately it is not always properly used. Some couples, at the time when they should be asking serious questions about their marriage prospects, avoid this altogether and give themselves little opportunity to explore the interpersonal levels of their relationship. Other couples, although they have deep misgivings about each other, ignore these warnings, taking refuge in such reassuring statements as, "It will all come right after we get married" or "When we settle down togther, I can make him over." Needless to say, these hopes are seldom fulfilled.

I recommend that you check together your personal experiences with the mate selection process as I have outlined it. Have you both graduated up through the system? Are you reasonably sure that you are being realistic in your judgments about your suitability to each other? Are there any areas of serious doubt or uncertainty that you should talk over with a counselor?

What Have You in Common?

Sociological studies, as we have seen, have shown that a good deal of compatibility in marriage is based on the fact that the couple came to each other with much in common. The general rule is that the more differences there are, the more adjustment they will have to make to each other. Let us look at some of the areas where difference could involve hazards.

Age: Modern marriages seem to work best for those who are about the same age, because this makes it more likely that their interests will be similar. An age difference in which the man is a few years older than the woman is the favored pattern, though a difference of up to as much as ten years may not cause problems. Likewise, marriages in which the woman is up to about five years older work well nowadays. Differences much greater than these should be looked at very carefully. There would need to be a lot of compensating advantages to justify such unions.

Social differences can bring strains. Being married to someone whose personal habits are very different from those you have accepted as normal can be exasperating, and if neither partner is comfortable with the relatives and friends of the other, this can also lead to serious complications.

Educational differences work very much the same way. This can be especially troublesome when one partner is *much* better educated than the other. If one partner corrects the grammar and emphasizes the ignorance of the other, hostility is likely to result.

What about religious differences? Interfaith marriages are common enough these days, and many of them succeed. Yet if the basic beliefs and loyalties of the couple are divided, a marriage will always tend to fall short of the ideal of "one heart, one mind." Problems can easily arise between the two families, particularly when there is conflict about the religious teaching of the children. Other things being equal, the interfaith marriage presents greater hazards, and is more likely to fail, than the union of two people of the same faith. This is equally true of a marriage between a deeply religious person and a partner who treats religion with indifference or contempt.

Interracial unions are increasing these days, though they still represent only a tiny minority of all marriages. Much evidence suggests that they involve special difficulties. When such marriages fail, this tends to confirm and support existing racial prejudices. It is probably best at the present time that such unions take place only between very mature people who have the resources necessary to make them succeed.

What about common tastes? This matters much less than common standards. But of course the companionship of husband and wife will be enhanced if they have the same basic ideas about the kind of house they want to live in, the kind of leisure activities they enjoy, the kind of people they like to meet. Differences here, however, need not be destructive. There should be enough flexibility in any marriage to allow husband and wife to arrive at compromises on relatively nonessential matters, and now and then to go their separate ways.

As part of your preparation for marriage, I would recommend that you go over your areas of common interest, list them, and see how much you can happily share together. Then focus on your areas of difference and disagreement, and find out how much enduring tolerance you can contribute to keeping the peace. All couples differ about some things, and this is not necessarily disastrous to a marriage. Where differences are many and deep, however, much tolerance is required.

What About Temperamental Differences?

People sometimes argue about whether married people get along best if they are alike, or whether there is something in the idea of the attraction of opposites. The truth seems to be that in good marriages we find both factors present. One formula which expresses this is "cultural similarity and emotional complementarity."

You will find it challenging, and I think fascinating, at this point to sit down together and ask each other: "What were the special things that attracted you to me? What needs of yours did you hope I would be able to meet?" Try writing down your answers to these questions separately first, without any collaboration, and then compare notes. I usually take time to get a couple involved in this kind of discussion.

Sexual attraction usually comes up right away. Of course this is important for people planning to marry; without it, I couldn't advise them to go ahead. But it is not a basis for marriage in itself, and should therefore not be at the top of the list. If it is, see that it is adequately supplemented by plenty of other favorable factors, or you may find yourselves in trouble.

What about dominance and submission? Some women unconsciously look for a strong, masterful, masculine husband. And some husbands feel a need to act protectively toward a wife who has strong dependency needs. But tread warily here. Aggressive males are often far from strong, and many a woman has been deceived on that score. Also, a wife who wants to lean on her husband all the time may become an intolerable burden to him, because he also has dependency needs. These supposed masculine-feminine differences are largely cultural stereotypes which we are giving up today. The marriage that works best nowadays is not a combination of strength and weakness, but a flexible companionship in which the dominance-submission roles can be switched when necessary.

What about the extrovert-introvert combination? On the whole it isn't a good one, because the principle of complementarity doesn't really apply. A man who likes a quiet life will not be helped by a wife who wants to give parties all the time, and the wife who is a homebody will languish if her husband spends all his evenings rushing from one committee to another. Two extroverts or two introverts usually find it easier to adjust to marriage, than a combination of both.

All the same, a strong factor in mate selection is the desire of each of you to be identified in some way with qualities in the other that you yourself seem to lack. It would be helpful to you both to understand how far this has contributed to bringing you together.

Acceptance and Tolerance of Each Other

What must be recognized is that living with each other's temperamental differences is one of the most difficult, and yet one of the most important, tests of a marriage. To be sensitive to each other's changes of mood, and where possible to be understanding and supportive, is the art of living together in harmony. All human beings suffer from fear and anger and self-distrust at times. And these are the testing times in a close relationship. If you can accept and succor each other at such times, you will tend to grow closer together in mutual interdependence. If at such times you reject each other, you will tend to drift apart.

This acceptance and tolerance of each other is already being tested in you as a couple seriously considering marriage. Your interpersonal encounter with each other doesn't begin when you marry. You are involved in it right now. Your similarities and differences are already manifesting themselves, now pulling you toward each other, now generating experiences of coolness which drive you apart. What I am asking you to do is to examine these experiences together and try to understand them. It is not always possible to do this at the time, because feelings can get too strong to be calmly or rationally expressed. But recognizing the feelings you generate in each other is highly important for the understanding of what is going on between you, and the understanding of what is going on between you is highly important for the growth of a relationship of mutual love and trust.

Today we are seeing compatibility in marriage not as a

state of affairs which is present from the beginning, but rather as a task to be achieved. No two people can reasonably expect to fit each other at every point. Even if they did, it might turn out to be a dull relationship. The lifelong task of marriage is to adapt continually to each other through a process of mutual growth and change.

Summary

Where are you now? Are you beginning to have some answers to this question? Can you now identify some of the things that are holding you together? Are there also things that are tending to drive you apart? All these need to be explored, understood, and dealt with if they call for appropriate action. This is the art of building a sound, wholesome relationship. You should find it stimulating and challenging. If you don't, maybe you need more help than you are able to give each other.

7

What Are Your Goals and Plans?

*O*n the process of looking at yourselves, you may have noticed that we began with your past, the influences in your individual lives that have shaped you. Then we considered your present, what is now going on between you. In this chapter, we shall turn to your future, what lies before you as a couple planning to marry.

Examine Your Expectations

Let's begin with your expectations. You have each developed, through the years, a kind of fantasy picture of what it will be like to be married, the joys and fulfillments you hope for. Since a great many difficulties in marriage develop because expectations are not fulfilled, now is the time to take a look together at your two separate blueprints.

The best way to do this is for each of you, without collaboration, to write out a statement on "what I am expecting from our marriage." It needn't be a long statement, but it should be quite specific. Vague generalities like "I want us to be very happy" won't help. You must really get down to the nitty-gritty details.

Now exchange these statements and plan a discussion session in which you can ask yourselves realistically how far your expectations are likely to be met. You'll probably have to do some revising of the blueprint. Some specifications will have to be altered, some scaled down, some even dropped (you will notice that I am likening this process to the joint building of your dream house, and it *is* rather like that).

Dreams and fantasies are all right. I believe in them. But we must be prepared to make concessions when we translate them into reality. This is particularly true of marriage, which we have idealized and romanticized to an excessive degree. As someone once expressed it, most of our complaints about marriage are based not on the fact that it is worse than the rest of human life, but that it is not infinitely better.

Some expectations, therefore, must be given up. Otherwise, you are going to be doomed to future disillusionment. However, to a reasonable extent, building castles in the air is all right. Thoreau said so—then he went on, "That is where they ought to be. Now build the foundations under them."

How do you do this? By setting your goals clearly, satisfying yourselves that they correspond to attainable reality, and then making plans to work progressively toward achieving them. To use the illustration of the dream house again, produce a blueprint on which you are both agreed, make sure that your particular house can be built on your chosen lot, and that the materials you would need for building it are available.

What Kind of Marriage for You?

In setting your goals, you will find yourselves having to decide what kind of marriage you really want. Marriages have been "typed" in many different ways. For your practical needs right now, let's confine ourselves to the question of the extent to which you really want, or are really able, to become involved in the sharing of each other's lives.

Marriage offers you many levels of mutual involvement, and we can summarize them under three headings.

There are the marriages of *minimum involvement*. I have already referred to these. Husband and wife enter into a kind of agreement to meet each other's needs by an exchange of services. He promises to provide maintenance for her and their children on a basis that represents the accepted standard within their social group. He will also perform the general duties of a husband and father, but not to an extent that would seriously interfere with his vocational goals or his hobbies. She, for her part, agrees to be sexually available to him at all reasonable times, to run the home, cook the meals, and raise the children. Beyond that, she will be free to pursue her own interests and to cultivate her friendships with other women.

This kind of marriage is quite common in our culture. You could probably name many couples who function on this basis. They don't normally "sign up" in advance for minimum involvement, and probably they are not even aware that this is the type of marriage they have chosen. But that is in fact what they have done, and they may be well satisfied. A marriage of this type makes few demands, and if this is all the husband and wife are expecting, there is a good chance that their expectations will be met.

In contrast with this is the marriage of *maximum involvement*. Idealistic couples may plunge eagerly for this, but they had better consider carefully what they are getting into. This is the marriage in which the couple decide to share their lives to the greatest possible extent. It implies a decision to live together in complete openness and honesty with each other, to devote themselves to working together for the same life goals, to attach equal importance to the personal needs and vocational aims of both partners, and not to favor one above the other. At the heart of this marriage lies the commitment to seek relationship-in-depth, the growth of the interpersonal relationship toward the realization, as nearly as possible, of its fullest potential.

It should be understood clearly that not many people are ready to pay the price of achieving this kind of marriage, nor does our culture favor it. Yet it is an ideal which some couples take seriously, and some—though only a few—attain it. William J. Lederer and Don D. Jackson, in *The Mirages of Marriage*, estimate that only about 5 to 10 percent of all couples achieve this kind of completely satisfying marriage, and this would seem to me to be a reasonable estimate.

For most couples the likely goal lies somewhere between these extremes, a marriage of *limited involvement*. They want to retain a good deal of individual freedom to go their own ways, but also they wish to enjoy a reasonable amount of togetherness. They are ready to be open to each other about most areas of their lives, but they want to reserve some territories which they do not share. They want to give the marriage a worthy place among their commitments but are not prepared to award it the top priority.

What is important is that you as a couple should try to set your goals together in advance. You should schedule a full discussion of this. Your goals needn't, of course, be rigidly set; you cannot know in advance what you are capable of achieving, but reaching some general agreement now could save you a lot of trouble later. The real tragedies occur when husband and wife, sometime after marriage, awaken to the realization that their goals and expectations for their life together, which they never really explored beforehand, turn out to be radically different and incapable of reconciliation. This is the time of disillusionment, of the shattering of the dreams.

The Inevitability of Conflict

It is well to recognize at the beginning in choosing your marital goals that the more involvement you decide for, the more effort is going to be required to fulfill your expectations. The marriage of minimal involvement makes very few demands on you. The marriage of maximum involvement will demand all you've got. Up and down the scale, the rule is that the more closeness and intimacy you seek, the greater the price you'll have to pay to get it.

Social psychologists help us to understand this by looking at relationships in terms of distance. If we imagine marriage as a box containing two people, their difficulties in living comfortably together will depend upon the size of the box. If it is a mile square, they needn't get too much involved. In times of tension, they can easily get out of shouting distance of each other. However, if you reduce the box to ten yards square, the situation is greatly changed. Living in that kind of closeness, if you do things that irritate each other, the distress suffered will be great, and the pain won't stop until you find a way to reduce the irritation.

Why then make the box so small? Because it is closeness and intimacy that we want and need. This is the great gift which marriage has to offer us. Sharing life in depth with another person is the solution to most of our human problems. It is in loving and being loved that we find the real meaning of life. Yet in seeking the closeness and intimacy that this involves, we inevitably generate conflict. This is our central human dilemma.

What this means is that the more you want to get out of marriage, the more conflict you will have to resolve in order to get it. For closeness emphasizes our differences, increases the possibilities of disagreement, and generates the heat of conflict. It would be true to say that *no close relationship can be achieved and maintained in any other way than by resolving the conflict which it inevitably produces.*

At whatever level you set your marital goals, some conflict will have to be dealt with. You must be having some right now, as an engaged couple. It is true that some couples, having very flexible and tolerant dispositions, generate less conflict or are able to handle conflict much more easily than others; but it must also be recognized that the couples who have little conflict are not necessarily those who achieve the best marriages. A relationship free of conflict may be so because it is really a superficial relationship. Some of the best marriages I have ever encountered have been those of couples who have confided to me that they have been through seas of trouble—"blood and sweat and toils and tears," said one husband, quoting Winston Churchill. But he went on to say that the struggle they had been through together had not only enabled the conflicts to be resolved but had also led them both to value deeply the good relationship they had achieved at so great a cost.

Communication and Cooperation

The task of achieving a good marriage will make many demands on you as a couple and will probably require some years of effort. It should be effort highly rewarded, but this will happen only if you go about it in the right way. Some couples expend enormous effort in trying to deal with their problems of mutual adjustment, yet the effort is in vain, because they use the wrong methods.

There are two means that together provide the sovereign remedy for most of the ills of marriage. They are *communication* and *cooperation*. Both are needed, because neither gets us very far without the other; although, fortunately, each tends to facilitate the other.

I believe it would be true to say that the task of marriage counseling involves, very largely, working with married couples in trouble with the objective of improving their communication and increasing their cooperation. This sounds easy. In fact, it is often very difficult.

In a close relationship, two people are all the time acting on each other, reacting to each other, and interacting with each other. That is the very nature of relationship—messages, verbal and nonverbal, are shuttling back and forth all the time. As long as these messages are interpreted as pleasant and friendly and supportive, husband and wife are happy and all goes well. But as soon as something negative or critical comes over from your partner, you react, you feel pain, you tense up and become defensive, you probably send back a negative message expressing your disapproval. Your partner may have known that the original message was negative and not be surprised to get a negative response. But the negativeness may have hurt you much more than your spouse expected, and the forcefulness of your response may have hurt so much that he or she sends back a more strongly negative message than the last time. Or your spouse may not have even known that the original message would be interpreted by you as negative, because it wasn't intended that way, and is now angry with you because of your misjudgment. So back comes an expression of annoyance.

You must surely recognize what I am describing. This kind of negative exchange between two people can happen quite easily and can start quite innocently. If it is often repeated, it develops into what I call a negative interaction spiral—one negative message being hurled back in response to another, and the process repeated like an exchange of artillery fire. When a couple get embattled in this kind of destructive process, it can alienate them seriously from each other. It becomes impossible to tolerate closeness, and they move away from each other till they get out of earshot.

This leads to a total breakdown of communication, which makes the situation worse because there is no possibility of mutual explanation of how it all got started. In this state of distance and tension, any attempt to restore closeness can easily start off another negative interaction spiral. So the relationship degenerates from bad to worse.

The best way of avoiding this kind of destructive erosion of the relationship is to keep the lines of communication open. A negative exchange can be stopped if one partner, instead of firing back another salvo, can say, "Look, we are in conflict. Can't we call a halt, calm down, and try to understand why we are doing this to each other?" This isn't easy, because angry people are not usually very rational. However, if the lines of communication are open, the first possible opportunity should be seized, after both have cooled down, to go over the whole experience, analyze what really happened, and take whatever action is needed to lessen the chance that the same thing will happen again.

What do I mean by "keeping the lines of communication open?" I mean agreeing to share negative feelings whenever they arise, without bitterness if possible. For instance, you could say, "Honey, you've done something that makes me mad, and I don't want to be mad with you. If I tell you about it, will you help me to understand just why I feel so hostile?" This may not always work, but it often will. The principle is, try not to swallow or bury any of your negative feelings (of which you will generate plenty) toward each other, but bring them out into the light of understanding. If all married couples learned to do just that, they would put most marriage counselors out of business.

Keep Working Toward Your Goal

Honest communication opens the way for cooperation. This must follow. If you just unload your negative feelings, that will give you only temporary relief. It is necessary to probe the situation till you really understand it, and then to experiment together till you find the way to adjust to each other so that it can't happen again.

Whatever marriage goals you set, the way to realize them is to keep communicating. Tolerate no misunderstanding between you. Misunderstanding breeds resentment, resentment produces hostility, and hostility starts the negative interaction spiral. Stop it at its source.

Nothing I can offer you will help you more than to learn the habit of examining your negative feelings to each other. Use your quarrels to practice this art. Go back over what happened, share with each other how you felt, discover the root of the difference between you, and find a way of digging it out. Do this over and over again in every negative exchange in which you become involved. Turn all your negative interactions into positive interactions. If you can do this, with or without counseling help, the goal of a mutually satisfying relationship is within your reach.

Part
Three

Marriage

What You Must Do to Succeed

8

How to Live with Sex

*I*f you were really making that trip to Africa, you would want to learn something in advance about where you were going. You'd study a map to see what the territory was like—mountains here, plains there, rivers flowing to the sea. You'd look at the political divisions on the map, the various countries and their capital cities. You would read a few books describing what life is like in Africa—the climate, the customs of the people, what to see, what to eat, what to wear.

In this section of our book we are going to do something like that. Preparing for marriage, as I have already stressed, is concerned less with facts than with feelings, with how you need to act rather than with what you need to know. But getting to know the facts is part of it too. So what I want to do at this point is to discuss with you some of the aspects of married life that give people trouble and that you should know about in order to be prepared. All I can do in very limited space is to emphasize a few of the major marital adjustments that seem to me, after a generation of marriage counseling, to be of central importance. If you want to explore this kind of thing further, there are plenty of good books to read, and I have prepared for you a selected list with some guidance about what they contain.

As we try to understand what married life is all about,

why not start with sex? After all, without it, there would be no marriage at all.

Our New Understanding of Sex

A generation ago, the main purpose of marriage preparation was to make sure that the engaged couple knew the "facts of life." The ignorance in which young people were allowed to grow up in those days seems incredible as we look back on it. Young women really went into marriage with only the vaguest idea of where babies come from. Young men, especially those from strict religious homes, were sometimes almost completely ignorant about female anatomy and physiology, and had to find out how to function sexually by a process, often painful, of trial and error. To the less sensitive young husband, marriage meant the opportunity to satisfy his sexual desires without restraint, and his young wife was expected to tolerate submissively whatever he did. The idea that the husband had a duty to make the experience pleasurable for his wife never entered his head. Few people had ever heard of the wife's sexual orgasm. I can recall counseling with a *physician* who, when I explained to him that a woman could reach a climax in sexual intercourse very similar to that of her husband, was completely astounded. He had never imagined such a thing.

As knowledge about sexual functioning began to spread, the "marriage manuals" began to be published. These books described the sex organs, internal and external, in detail and then went on to explain what happened in sexual intercourse. It became the fashion for couples about to marry to be given one of these books by their physician or pastor. Great emphasis was placed upon sexual technique, which explained to the husband-to-be, step by step, how to arouse his wife so that she could share his enjoyment of their sexual relationship. The books were quite helpful, especially to those who would otherwise have entered marriage in almost complete ignorance. But what they had to say was, for too many couples, too little and too late. Those of us who were pioneers in marriage counseling in those early days knew only too well how many marriages were in trouble on account of all kinds of sexual difficulties. A physician who worked with me for many years in London, England, and specialized in the treatment of sexual disharmony, estimated that as many as 90 percent of all wives were unable to achieve orgasm. He proved to be quite wrong about this. But from the point of view of his practice, the steady stream of unhappy wives who sought his help seemed to justify his gloomy estimate.

Much has happened since those days, and we have made great progress in our understanding of sexual functioning. We tend to think of the sexual revolution in terms of an increase in premarital sex, and that is certainly true. But the really revolutionary thing that has happened has been the new understanding of sex that has come to married people. A rough estimate shows that, every twenty-four hours in the United States, some thirty million people have sexual intercourse. The overwhelming majority of these are married couples, and there can be no doubt that a remarkable transformation has taken place in their freedom to enjoy the physical expression of their love.

You who marry today may consider yourselves fortunate to be living in an era of enlightenment about this important aspect of marriage. The information that was so hard to get a generation ago is now common knowledge. In this book on marriage preparation, it seems unnecessary to devote more than one chapter to sex.

However, we had better not be too enthusiastic about the changes that have taken place, because our troubles are not entirely over. Married couples still come to me with sexual difficulties, mainly premature ejaculation and impotence in men, orgasm inadequacy in women. Masters and Johnson, whose researches have revolutionized our ideas about some areas of sexual functioning, suggest in their book *Human Sexual Inadequacy* that as many as half of all married couples may still experience some trouble in achieving sexual adjustment, although they add more hopefully that sexual inadequacy could be almost eliminated in the coming years.

Preparing for Marital Sex

What you are concerned about as a couple moving into marriage is what you can do to ensure that this important area of your relationship will be satisfying to you both. Here are five areas for you to consider separately and then discuss together in a joint session:

1. *Check your own sex education to make sure it is adequate.* Sex education in the schools has been a long time coming, and it suffered some setbacks when it did begin to be developed. It is probably certain, therefore, that you had no formal teaching on the subject that could be called anything like adequate. You have had to do your own private study of the subject, prompted by natural curiosity.

Now is the time to check your knowledge, because this is a subject of primary importance for married people. Sex education normally covers four fields. You should have a reasonably clear understanding of the process of human reproduction and of the various methods of contraception. You should know the basic facts about the structure of the male and female sex organs and about sexual functioning. You should have enough knowledge about sexual ethics to have established for yourself an acceptable code of personal behavior. Finally, you should have some comprehension of the basic psychology of masculine and feminine attitudes and responses. These can all become vast subjects if studied in detail, and this is not at all necessary. But an elementary knowledge of all these areas is essential equipment for married life. Books covering this material are included in the list provided for your guidance.

2. *Make sure that your own individual attitudes to sex are sound and healthy.* You have already made an evaluation of your past sexual experiences and how they have affected you. What is important now is to clear up any negative associations with sex which produce anxiety or guilt. You should feel comfortable and positive about your sexual nature and about the feelings and desires it stirs within you. There should be nothing here to be ashamed of or afraid of. If there is, it would be great wisdom for you to seek professional help about it. You owe it to your partner not to go into marriage unhappy, disturbed, or anxious about sex.

3. *Establish open communication between you about sexual feelings and responses.* Advice of this kind would not have been considered proper a generation ago. Today I offer it without hesitation. Two people going into marriage ought to be able to talk to each other quite freely, without embarrassment, about the way they affect each other sexually. Awkwardness and concealment here create confusion and misunderstanding. You two people have decided to bestow your sexuality upon each other, to be shared fully and without reserve for the rest of your lives. This is not something to be evasive about.

Talking together about this may, in fact, help you both a great deal in coming to terms with your own individual sexuality. The atmosphere of loving confidence and acceptance that should exist between you can do much to take away sexual anxiety and guilt.

4. *Insist upon reaching full agreement about whatever sexual experiences you're having together now.* I simply assume that you are having sexual experiences of some sort, though not necessarily full sexual intercourse. The figures from our most recent researches suggest that the majority of all the women in this country now have premarital sexual intercourse by the time they reach the age of twenty-one. The number of boys experiencing premarital intercourse is decidedly higher than the number of girls. These figures have been steadily increasing during recent years.

I would certainly support any couple who decide that

waiting for marriage is the best plan for them. However, if we leave sexual intercourse on one side for a moment and consider petting and other sexual intimacies short of intercourse, we find that 99 percent of girls admit some involvement. So I conclude that practically all couples looking toward marriage are having some sort of sexual intimacies.

Exactly what you are doing together sexually is your own affair. All I am concerned about is what it may be doing to you. If you are both entirely happy about what is going on, free from any disquieting feelings, and blissfully contented with the pleasure you are giving each other, I have nothing more to say—unless you are taking risks that may lead to an undesired pregnancy. If, for example, you are having intercourse and not using a reliable contraceptive, you are taking chances, and in my opinion, acting irresponsibly. I don't happen to believe that a loving couple should conspire together to act irresponsibly, because this is very poor preparation for marriage.

Another thing I am concerned about is to make sure that one of you isn't in any way exploiting the other. This can easily happen, and it can be deeply damaging to your relationship. The usual situation is that he persuades her—against her better judgment—to have intercourse, though she would rather not do so. This is an unloving act, and it is made all the more hypocritical when he suggests to her that she is proving her love for him by letting him have his way. A woman treated in this fashion can easily develop a smoldering resentment that breaks down her confidence and trust in the man she loves. Anything of this kind—any taking advantage of each other to gain your sexual ends—is a dangerous misuse of sex that could spoil it for both of you in the end.

Sex is sheer enjoyment when fully shared by a loving couple. But it can become a destructive force in their relationship when one partner allows personal need to get out of control and imposes his or her will on the other. Handling sexual responses sensitively and sympathetically is not easy, but it is essential to a good sex life in marriage. If the management of sex before marriage sometimes puts self-control to a severe test, meeting that test successfully will strengthen your confidence. It will prove to you that you will be able, equally well, to cope with other situations that may arise in which, for love's sake, you have to forego having your own way. The capacity to consider the needs and wishes of the other as much as your own is of all qualities the one that matters most in marriage.

5. *Put the emphasis always on sex as experience and not as performance.* Our new knowledge of patterns of sexual response, while valuable in itself, has had one disturbing result. People are in danger of becoming upset if they fail to measure up to certain standards of performance and of judging each other in terms of whether or not they measure up. For many this has taken most of the joy and spontaneity out of sex and turned it into work rather than play. What is particularly distressing about this is that, when we turn sex into work and effort, it may respond by refusing to cooperate. At the root of nearly all the so-called psychosexual difficulties is the association of anxiety with sexual performance.

Each couple's sex life is something uniquely personal to them alone. Americans are a highly competitive people, but in this most private area there is really no need to try to keep up with the Joneses. Calculating frequencies of intercourse and counting orgasms may be appropriate for researchers, but for married couples it can have devastating results. I could tell harrowing stories of grimly serious husbands consumed with anxiety because their wives didn't have what some book had said was the correct number of orgasms, and of outraged wives who complained that their husbands wanted to experiment with some daring departure from what has been called "the missionary position." One very wise and experienced physician gave a clear answer on this latter point. "Whatever is physiologically sound," he declared, "is also ethically right." In other words, as long as you break no bones, it's OK.

9

How to Treat Your In-laws

$\mathcal{S}$omeone once came up with a simple answer to this problem. "Outlaw the in-laws," he declared. Many of us would have to confess that there have been times when we have wished that we could do just that. But it wouldn't solve anything.

We have already discussed how you are each a product of your family background. The influence of your parents is not something you can cast off. It is part of you, built into your personality at deep, unconscious levels. So even if you rebel against them, even if you repudiate them and treat them as strangers, they are still there, influencing your judgments and controlling your behavior. Any psychotherapist can confirm this for you. It is a fact established on the basis of mountains of evidence. You had better accept it.

In-law Problems Can Be Complicated

The implications of this for married couples are profound and far-reaching. There are no serious problems when both of you enjoy excellent relationships with your respective parents, your parents accept your marriage partner wholeheartedly, and the two sets of parents get along famously together. In these happy circumstances, there is agreement all round, and the in-laws lend their support to the married couple and give them a deep sense of security. This is the ideal arrangement, and it is not rare or exceptional. Many families have this sense of solidarity. When Dr. Evelyn Duvall made her study of in-law problems, she found that 25 percent of all the married couples she approached reported that they could make no useful contribution to the study because their relationships with their in-laws were excellent and they had no problems at all.

However, problems often do arise. The ideal situation I have described is obviously the result of a fortunate combination of circumstances. Often enough this doesn't happen. There is a great deal that can go wrong. So let's look at the other side of the picture.

Sometimes everything goes wrong. Suppose both of you are in a state of strained relations with your parents, and the two sets of parents are not on speaking terms with each other. That would represent a situation full of conflict. Such situations are not rare or exceptional either. But apart from this extreme state of alienation all around, there can exist all sorts of intermediate groupings and alliances. If both of you are alienated from your parents, the parents on both sides may find a common bond in having rebellious children and join forces in an effort to bring you both to reason. Then it becomes a straight conflict between the generations. Or the parents on one side may sympathize with you both about the hard treatment the parents on the other side are handing out. It is not even unusual to find one marriage partner supported by the parents of the other, who reject the behavior of their own son or daughter.

Further complications can arise when the parents on one side, or even on both sides, are divided among themselves. Sometimes a mother will support her son while the father takes the side of his daughter-in-law. Or it may happen the other way round.

I have surely said enough to make it clear that this can be a very prickly problem area. And the solution isn't to cut yourself off from the in-laws. Parents can be a powerful stabilizing force in a marriage, and it is worth making great efforts to gain their acceptance and support. Patience and perseverance in this task may pay off handsomely in the end.

Every couple who have in-law problems should develop a strategy for dealing with them. The shadow of future conflict, if not the conflict itself, usually appears unmistakably on the horizon during the premarriage period. Sometimes this even proves to be the worst time of all, and the situation gets better after marriage. Sometimes the reverse is true.

A sound strategy must meet three basic requirements. First, it must be fully agreed upon and loyally acted upon by both of you. If one defaults, the strategy collapses and doesn't work. So your planning should be very thorough.

The second requirement is that the plan should be positive with the objective of achieving reconciliation and harmony, not retaliatory or punitive based on your angry and hurt feelings. The aim is not to reject the in-laws and shut them out of your lives, but if at all possible to win them over and create an atmosphere of mutual confidence and trust.

The third requirement is that your strategy should take account of the realities of the situation. These you should study carefully together. No two in-law problems are exactly alike. Yet there are frequently recurring factors that are common to most of them.

The Core of the Problem

Let me list the main facts about in-law tensions for your guidance in working out your own plan of campaign.

1. The person who causes most of these conflicts is unfortunately the husband's mother. One study found that she initiated as much trouble as all the other in-laws put together. Fathers-in-law usually stay in the background, though sometimes they come helpfully to the rescue.

2. The victims of in-law interference are nearly always the daughters-in-law. It was from them, in the study I have mentioned, that nine out of ten of the complaints came. What most often happens is that the mother-in-law is jealous of her daughter-in-law for dividing the affection of her son and tries to win back her central position in his life by alienating him from his wife. Unfortunately he sometimes finds it flattering to be the object of competition, and fails to take a firm stand against his mother's interference.

3. The competition and conflict between these two women reaches its most violent form when they have to live together in the same home. Doubling up with in-laws, if there is any likelihood of conflict, should therefore be firmly avoided. It just places too much strain on everyone concerned.

4. Another area in which the mother-in-law frequently interferes is in the raising of the children. She does this by questioning their mother's child-rearing policies or tries to buy the affection of the children by indulging them with gifts and special privileges.

5. The mother-in-law who acts in these ways can be very troublesome. But you should never lose sight of the fact that she is almost certainly more deserving of your pity than of your hostility. Again and again she turns out to be a very unhappy person. The typical example is a woman who never managed to develop a really close and mutually supportive relationship with her husband and sought emotional fulfillment instead in caring for her children. Now that they are leaving her, she tries desperately to regain their attention and to get them back into her power. At the same time she is aware that she is beginning to grow old, and she may also be going through the emotional upheavals of menopause. She sees little to look forward to in her future and therefore embarks on a campaign to achieve a sense of personal worth by gaining power over others. Most of this is done unconsciously—she is not aware of her own motivations. What she really needs is the love of those around her, but since she seems

unable to get it she tries instead to gain her ends by manipulation and intrigue. Unfortunately she usually doesn't realize that she is completely defeating her own purpose.

A Strategy for Avoiding Needless Conflict

Let me add now some working principles that have helped other couples to meet their in-law problems.

1. No in-law interference can damage a sound marriage. When husband and wife have an agreed policy and stand firmly together in putting it into effect, in-law attempts at exploitation and manipulation invariably fail. But any weakness, any crack in the unity of husband and wife, enables the in-laws to drive a wedge between them.

2. The policy to adopt is to make it clear that you want to be friendly and work for harmony between the generations, but that you simply will not tolerate unwarranted interference in your marriage. This must be made unmistakably clear and no compromise tolerated. Sometimes this can only be done in a painful, out-in-the-open, once-and-for-all confrontation. When the in-laws have thus been shown decisively that their interference will not be tolerated, they usually give up and accept the situation.

3. This decisive confrontation should be followed up by sincere and genuine attempts to be friendly and conciliatory. Even if you simply don't like your in-laws as persons (and that isn't your fault), you can act kindly toward them. We can all manage to be pleasant to people who are not congenial to us when we have to meet them socially or do business with them. Surely we can do at least that much in the cause of family unity. Many people make the mistake of thinking that if you have little in common with your in-laws, there is nothing you can do about it. In fact, you can behave lovingly even if you don't feel loving, and the action tends to promote the feeling. It will help and

encourage your partner if you make a real and successful effort in this direction. Experience shows that this policy can in time achieve a surprising degree of success.

4. If you and your in-laws really have very little in common, the best way to maintain good relationships is to visit them from time to time, but always keep the visits brief. A congenial atmosphere can usually be maintained for a reasonably short period of time, particularly if you are all involved in doing something interesting together. But if you stay together too long with nothing much to do, tensions may arise and goodwill may deteriorate rapidly.

5. Always remember that family ties cannot be broken but last throughout a lifetime. Even if your relationships with your in-laws are not very congenial right now, a time may come when you may need their help or they may need yours. In the significant events of life, family members usually get together and participate; and in the crises of life, it is to them that we have the natural right to turn. You cannot predict what the future will bring. The bonds that seem unimportant now may one day become a lifeline to you or to your children. It is wisdom to bend over backward if necessary in order to keep the family relationships in good repair.

10

How to Manage Your Money

*T*he United States is the richest country in the world. Yet when someone organizes a quiz to find out what problems give Americans the most trouble in marriage, financial difficulties have a habit of heading the list. Why is this?

There are probably many reasons. One is that in an affluent society people feel confident they'll always be able to get what they want in one way or another, so they don't have the fear of starvation chilling their spines and making them careful. Another is that Americans, perhaps as a result of the barrage of clever advertising to which they are continually exposed, put a greater value on possessing things than do some of the older cultures. Yet another reason is that many Americans today have been brought up on the principle that whenever you want something you get it, even if you run into debt in the process. In one way and another we are tremendous consumers. In relation to the size of our population, we use up a vast proportion of the world's resources.

Money as a Status Symbol

Financial trouble in marriage, however, doesn't just reflect the national spending habits. It always has a deeper personal significance. In the poorer cultures money represents the means of survival. But in our culture, where so many people have far more than they need in order to survive, it has also become an important status symbol. You measure your self-worth in terms of the amount and quality of the goods you are able to buy. Each of you already has developed a certain concept of what kind of expenditure is appropriate to your worth as a person. You know the kind of house and the kind of neighborhood that would be right for you to live in, the kind of car you ought to drive, the kind of restaurant you like to eat in. When your expenditure goes above what you consider to be appropriate, it makes you feel important, although at the same time you may also feel insecure. When your expenditure has to be on a lower scale than you feel you are entitled to, your self-esteem is wounded, and you feel outraged and insulted.

Two people may bring to marriage quite different standards, and this can cause plenty of trouble. As long as you are spending your own money, what you do with it is your business. But if you and I are going into partnership, strains can soon develop. If I feel that you are buying something we can't afford, I'm going to protest. On the other hand, if you deny me the right to buy what I think I am entitled to, I am going to protest even more vigorously. Obviously, there is ample scope for disagreements here, and they are apt to be bitter disagreements, because they touch us in a very sensitive area—that of our self-esteem.

The use of money, therefore, puts the partnership of marriage to one of its severest tests. So, unless you are in the fortunate position of having almost unlimited financial resources (and even then, your spending habits will tend to creep up till they reach the ceiling), you simply have to have an agreed policy. What money management really does is to test a couple's capacity to organize their joint life in a rational and orderly fashion—and surprising as it may seem, this is something most of us find peculiarly difficult.

Some Guidelines for a Financial Policy

I therefore suggest that, as part of your preparation for marriage, you work out together a plan that expresses your areas of agreement about financial policies, and I urge you particularly to look into any questions about which you are unable to reach agreement. To help you to get started, let me offer some suggestions that others have found helpful and that you might want to consider. Here is an outline of the issues in family finances on which you will have to make decisions if you are to have a workable policy.

1. *Do you favor joint sharing?* Some married couples keep their own money separately and do not hold each other accountable for the way in which they spend it. The old-fashioned husband, quite often, didn't even tell his wife how much he earned. He doled out her weekly "housekeeping money" and kept the rest of his pay package. She had to meet all personal expenses out of "housekeeping" or persuade her husband to give her any additional items she needed. Sometimes this was so humiliating that she built up a secret nest egg to give herself a sense of independence.

The modern method is joint sharing. This means you both should know all about the assets you jointly hold and the debts you jointly owe. Without this basis of shared knowledge you can't even begin to formulate a joint policy.

You should discuss how far you can both accept the principle that all your assets really belong to both of you and also accept all debts as a joint responsibility. Are you both ready to assume, and to let the other assume, equal responsibility for all financial decisions? If not, why not?

2. *Who will be the treasurer?* You will need to have a policy for the actual handling of financial transactions. Traditionally the husband always paid the bills. But nowadays the wife often does this, and the husband may be glad to be relieved of the responsibility. Some couples decide who will manage the money on the basis of who is better equipped for this task, regardless of sex. It is possible also, of course, for both to pay bills out of separate checking accounts or by writing checks on a joint account. If this policy is adopted, it is as well to have a clear understanding about the areas in which each is entitled to make

payments. Otherwise confusion may well arise. A bill may go unpaid because each thought the other took care of it, or a bill may even be paid twice over.

3. *What will your budget look like?* Working out a hypothetical budget is such a good way of discovering each other's basic attitudes to money management that I seriously suggest that you spend an evening or two together on it. I believe you would learn a great deal about each other in the process.

Begin by estimating as nearly as you can what your joint income might add up to. Then make estimates as accurately as you can of all the basic expenditures that would have to come out of this income: housing, utilities, furnishings, food, clothes, medical care, continuing education, personal items, automobile, vacation, insurance, savings, charities, and the like. Then see how income and expenditure are likely to balance out and how effectively you could manage to live within your income.

This cannot be done precisely, of course. So the exercise should not be taken too seriously. The aim is to find out how far you can reach agreement and where your areas of conflict in money management are likely to be. A good idea, when a group of couples is involved, is for each couple to work separately on their budget and then for all to meet for a general discussion of the principles and methods of money management.

4. *What about personal allowances?* One of the most perplexing questions in the area of family finance is how to deal with small personal items such as haircuts, drinks, cigarettes, hobbies, gifts, movies, and such. To put so many small items into a budget is both tedious and time-consuming. They are hard to estimate in advance, and most of us thoroughly dislike having to make an entry in a notebook every time we buy a postage stamp or put a dime in a parking meter.

The best solution to this problem seems to be to give all members of the family (including children when they are old enough) an individual personal allowance, weekly or monthly, which they can use for these small items, and for which they don't have to keep records. Finding out how much represents a fair allowance can be done only by experiment, and you have to be flexible about this until you get it right. The system, however, seems to work better than any other. If the wife doesn't earn any of the family income, it is good for her to have an allowance that she can really call her own. And having a regular weekly allowance helps children at an early age to learn the value of money and how to manage it wisely.

It is necessary to decide just what range of items is to be bought out of these personal allowances. This usually includes recreation. Some families make it big enough to include clothes as well. Other families budget separately for clothes, and at least for recreation in which all share together.

5. *What is your attitude toward debt?* In the time of our grandparents the custom was to pay cash down, and it was considered disgraceful to get into debt, except for such major items as a mortgage on the family home. Now all that has changed, and many people buy most major items—furniture, cars, appliances, and the like—on the basis of payment with interest extended over a period of time. Charge accounts and credit cards are becoming more and more widely accepted, and the total of the nation's individual indebtedness is reaching astronomic figures. We are even told that it is good for the economy for us to buy now and pay later.

There is another side to this. Families on marginal incomes often get into serious trouble by using this system. Married couples have endless quarrels about how to meet the mounting total of monthly payments and to buy food to eat as well. Often the amount of interest paid out consumes a sizable proportion of a weekly paycheck. And when the facts are realistically faced, many of the goods purchased really were not needed at all.

Most married couples have to decide firmly, sooner or later, where to take a stand on this question of debt. It could prevent a lot of later misery if you could agree on a sound policy now.

6. *What are your insurance needs?* Insurance makes good sense and brings peace of mind. But we need so much of it these days that the overcautious can easily find themselves "insurance poor." There are life insurance, health insurance, home insurance, and automobile insurance, for a start. Then you can go on to accident insurance, disability insurance, and many others. Where do you stop?

Insurance needs have to be seen in proportion, in relation to each other and in relation to available income. For example, a young husband starting out with small income and heavy expenses would be well advised to buy term insurance to cover his life and switch to ordinary life later. There are flexible plans available for almost every possible situation, but you have to know about them and understand them, or you can make foolish mistakes.

7. *Do you plan to buy a house?* Real estate costs have soared to alarming heights these days, and many young couples feel that home ownership is right out of their reach. Yet having a place you can call your own brings to a family one of its deepest and most lasting satisfactions. Buying a home is also a good way of building up savings, because if it is a good house in a good neighborhood, its value should go up steadily, and it would be a salable item in a dire emergency. On the other hand, if the breadwinner's job calls for the possibility of a number of moves, renting an apartment could be a better plan. You should weigh these issues carefully in the light of your personal prospects.

In the old days, married couples were usually content to start housekeeping with a few inexpensive items of furniture and equipment and to replace these later when there was a little more money in the bank. Nowadays, many newly married couples feel that they must have a houseful of brand new, high-quality equipment from the start, and in order to achieve this they put themselves under a crippling burden of debt. You should consider seriously what policy makes sense for you.

8. *What about savings?* A recent magazine article described a family that had a total income of forty thousand dollars a year, yet the couple reported that it was absolutely impossible for them to save a cent. What hope is there for those of us who have to live on far less than that?

The answer is that it depends on your philosophy of life. I have known couples who have had to deny their children educational opportunities that would have launched them on successful professional careers, simply because they had squandered money earlier on needless luxuries. And I have seen elderly people end their days in tragic squalor because in their carefree youth they took no thought for the morrow.

The average married couple, in addition to meeting their day-to-day expenses, need during their lifetime to plan savings for three major purposes. First, they should aim at owning a home of their own someday. Second, they will need the means to provide their children with a good education. Third, they will need resources for their retirement years. It is well to face these contingencies from the very beginning and to have a sound plan to meet them. I know that most of us are helped in these days by compulsory forms of saving like Social Security and pension plans. But these usually provide only a basic amount and need to be supplemented if we want to enjoy anything like the standard of living to which we have grown accustomed.

A savings policy means an investment policy, and there we are in a very complex field in which I cannot claim to be qualified to guide you. What you need here is the advice of a well-informed person who is not going to sell you anything—the man with something to sell will naturally wish to direct your thoughts toward the merits of his product. Be cautious, too, about accepting the advice of your personal friends or colleagues whose knowledge of investing may be no more reliable than their own limited experience.

Summary

Happy indeed are those who never have a disagreement about money. The best way to join their ranks is to discuss the whole question thoroughly now and to reach if possible an agreed policy on the various aspects of the subject which I have raised with you.

Remember, however, that money itself is not the trouble. Money is simply a useful device to facilitate the exchange of goods and services. Your quarrels and disagreements on financial matters are always the reflection of conflict in your relationship. Don't, therefore, be satisfied with solutions in terms of money policy alone. Try always to get behind the money itself to the reasons why you are using it as a battleground. Clear up the underlying conflicts, and with a basic amount of sound knowledge and good judgment you will be able to handle your financial affairs satisfactorily.

11

A Few More Problem Areas

A wise old social worker once said to me, "Marriage problems? I've been dealing with them all my life. If you ask me, they all boil down to three problem areas: sex, in-laws, and money."

These are the problem areas we have discussed so far, and they certainly are the ones about which most married people seem to need help. But there are plenty of other problem areas. I don't see any need to give you a long list of them, because you are not exactly looking for trouble. However, there are a few that you ought to know about, and I will draw your attention to them, quite briefly, in this chapter.

Children

The blessing of parenthood has always been highly prized, and having children is normally a great joy to a husband and wife. Yet this area of married life can cause trouble too.

Few people ever try to analyze their reasons for wanting children. If they did, they would find quite a variety of motives. The wish to perpetuate your identity, keep up with the neighbors, prove your manhood or womanhood, provide someone to care for you in your old age—these are some of the motives which we don't generally acknowledge. You might like to talk this over together. Do you both really want children? What are your main reasons? Are you substantially in agreement about this? You had better be. Unresolved conflict in this area can be very painful.

How many children would you like to have? The days of the big family seem to be about over. Studies suggest that two children is the number most often wanted nowadays. But since the population problem has been brought so prominently to our attention, some people are deciding to have none at all. What is your view about this?

Then there is the matter of spacing the children in a family. I assume you will get some sound advice from your physician about birth control, and I need not discuss this in detail. But you still must make some decisions. Will you try to start a family right away after marriage? Or do you follow the school of thought that advocates waiting a year or so, either to make your early marital adjustments without the complications of pregnancy, or so that you can accumulate a capital reserve from your earnings. There are good arguments on both sides, and I wouldn't want to influence you either way.

What if you should want children, but none come? Then you should ask your doctor for a full checkup on your fertility. Both of you should be tested. These days, it is usually possible to locate the trouble, and in many cases it can be cleared up. If it cannot be, you have to choose between an adoption, artificial insemination if it is the husband who is sterile, or a childless marriage. The latter choice needn't be a tragedy. It may surprise you to know that, according to some studies, childless marriages prove to be a shade happier than those with children.

Conflicts over raising the children arise in many marriages. But we counselors find that this is usually a projection of conflicts already present between the couple. The coming of children, according to the findings of many researchers, intensifies the existing state of the marriage. If the couple are happy together, children tend to increase that happiness. If the marriage is unhappy, children unfortunately are likely to make it more so.

Work

Married people labor in two fields, in the home and outside it. The traditional pattern was that the wife took care of the housework while the husband went out and earned the money.

That pattern has changed a great deal. In fact, there is no clear pattern anymore. So you will have to work out your own. If the wife is going to be employed, will the husband help out at the homemaking end? Some men don't like domestic duties. Yet the wife naturally feels let down if she works in both spheres, and her husband works in only one.

Another factor is that some husbands feel it to be a reflection on their masculinity if they can't support their wives, and they resent the wife's wanting to take an outside job. Yet the wife often needs the job not just to earn money but also to feel that she is doing something significant in the world and putting her education and training to good use. If she stays at home, she may suffer from what Margaret Mead once called the "trapped housewife syndrome."

Then there is the question of whether a mother who goes out to work is neglecting her children. It was once thought that children suffered severely when the mother was absent for part of the day. Now we know that with really adequate day care and wise use of the time when the mother is at home, the children need not suffer at all. Some argue that they will actually be better off because a mother who goes out into the world will be better equipped to guide her children as they go out into the world.

There are pros and cons on all these questions. If the issue is one that is likely to concern you, it would be wise to discuss it thoroughly before marriage and reach agreement about the policy you favor.

Friends

During this period you naturally want to spend a lot of time by yourselves. But once you are married, the question of your social life has to be decided. Many a man takes the view that once he has won his fair lady and settled her in a home, he can return to his own cronies and spend most of his spare time with them. But the wife may not see it in this light, so there is trouble. If he persists, she may establish her own separate social life, and before long they are drifting apart.

While former associates need not be dropped, it helps a marrige if husband and wife can build new friendships on a couple basis. When people get married they cross a sort of invisible line. The focus of their life changes, they develop new interests, and it becomes inappropriate to go back to the old carefree bachelor patterns. If both can make the transition smoothly together, all will be well. But if one is ready to make it and the other isn't, there can be trouble.

Then there's the knotty question of friends of the opposite sex. Jealousy can cause havoc between married couples, and you need to have a clear understanding about how you both regard such friendships in any depth. In these swinging days of spouse-swapping, some couples seem to be very permissive about such matters. It is dangerous, however, to assume that any but a small minority of people take this point of view.

Married couples certainly need to have their circle of friends. "Two people wrapped up in each other," someone has said, "make a very small parcel." But the choice of these friends, the activities shared with them—these questions need to be settled with the full agreement of both of you.

Recreation

One aspect of the question of outside friends is the use of leisure time. Some couples have common interests and like to spend their evenings together pursuing their hobbies. Usually this is good for their marriage. It avoids the danger that otherwise all their time together might have to be devoted to household chores, making routine decisions, and coping with family problems.

However, when the leisure interests of husband and wife take them in opposite directions, what then? To a reasonable extent, by common agreement, they can live with this. If they can get each other interested in their respective pursuits, they can at least report on their significant experiences afterward without boring each other. But sometimes the point comes at which individual sacrifices must be made for the sake of the marriage. I remember my own personal predicament in a situation of this kind when I found soon after marriage that my wife was feeling lonely and neglected on Saturday afternoons when I left her to play my favorite ball game. This disturbed me, and I finally dropped out of the team. Instead we started going for long country hikes together on Saturday afternoons, which we both enjoyed very much.

The question of vacations comes up here, also. Some people like to seek the life of the city, others prefer the solitude of the mountains. Some love to travel abroad, some feel more secure at home. Some love camping, some hate it. When two people marry with radically different preferences, what do they do? I think an occasional separate vacation is a reasonable compromise, but to make a habit of it may lead to complications.

Leisure hours are coming these days to add up to a lot of total time. Planning to use it wisely may be an important contribution to the success of your marriage.

Personal Habits

We are always being told the story of the marriage that broke up because the husband insisted that the bedroom window should be open all night and the wife was equally determined to keep it closed. It isn't really true that such differences can break a marriage. It is the immovable stubbornness in both that makes it impossible for them to live together. And if they slept in a bedroom with no windows at all, they would find something else to fight about.

If minor irritants of this kind don't break marriages, however, they certainly can wear down goodwill and cool affection. An otherwise loving wife who disapproves of alcohol is going to be anything but loving when the husband comes home drunk. A husband who thinks smoking is an unpleasant and unhealthy habit isn't going to be motivated to kiss his wife when she reeks of tobacco. The husband who has to catch the 7:10 to the office each morning is going to get pretty crabby if his wife keeps him up talking till midnight, and the compulsively tidy housewife will be exasperated by the husband who leaves his discarded clothes lying all over the bedroom and bathroom floor.

Some annoying personal habits usually show up before marriage, and that's a good time to face them squarely. Otherwise the annoyance will certainly be intensified in the closer and more continuous shared life of marriage. Most of your personal habits are not ingrained, and you should be willing to change them, or at least modify them to please the one you love most. Unwillingness to accommodate yourself in these matters may be interpreted as meaning that you don't care; and if you don't care, the next question is how much do you really love? People who expect to go into marriage without making any changes in their living patterns just don't understand what marriage is all about. If we say we love each other, the best proof of it is our willingness to try hard to be pleasing in the way we behave.

Summary

I have given you some examples of the adjustments to each other that married people have to be willing to make in order to live happily and harmoniously together. You don't need to take all of them too seriously because many may never arise in your particular case, but you will have adjustments to make and some of them will be irksome. This fact you had better understand clearly.

There are two good reasons why you should spend some time now, before you marry, in trying to identify some of your potential problem areas. The first is that by knowing in advance what the task of marriage is likely to involve, you will be spared the shattering sense of letdown you might otherwise suffer when the discouraging realities can no longer be evaded. By preparing for them ahead of time, you will be equipped with well-formulated policies to deal with them when that time comes.

The other reason for facing these issues now is that you really don't have to wait till marriage to make all of these adjustments to each other. Some adjustment problems, I am sure, have already come up between you. Many couples adopt the philosophy of "have fun now, work later" and shelve the problems. You should consider whether this really is a good approach. If you do some of the work now, you can still have fun; and you will very much ease the later task of marital adjustment by doing some of your homework in advance.

12

Summing Up

*W*ell, that's it! I have now gone over with you both the questions I would have raised with you if you had actually come to me together for marriage preparation, and we had set up a series of interviews. I have not, of course, gone into medical questions that concern your physician or into religious questions which your pastor will discuss with you. But I have tried to give you basic marriage preparation which can be supplemented, according to your need, by reading to gain further information and by face-to-face counseling in some particular area.

I've given you a lot of homework to do, separately and together. Just by way of a final check, let me list the assignments I have suggested to you:

1. *Your Individual Marriageability.* To determine this, I asked each of you to make an individual self-evaluation covering nine areas which we went over in chapter 5. I asked you to do this separately in writing, then to meet, and—as far as you felt you could—to share your notes with each other.

2. *Your Compatibility as a Couple.* In chapter 6, I asked you to consider, separately and then together, the following areas: your personal experiences with the mate selection process, what you do and do not have in common, and your emotional complementarity.

3. *Your Marital Expectations.* In chapter 7, I suggested you should—again separately and then together—look at your goals and plans for your marriage; first, sharing lists of your individual expectations, then discussing what type of marriage, in terms of involvement, you both want; and finally using areas of disagreement to put in some practice in the all-important art of conflict resolution.

4. *Your Marital Adjustments.* Finally, I set you the task of looking ahead and trying to decide how you would handle together a whole series of adjustments you will have to make if your marriage is to succeed, and most of which you can begin working on now. Specifically, I gave you the following items for discussion: your sexual attitudes (chapter 8); your in-law strategy (chapter 9); your financial policy (chapter 10); your approach to parenthood, your division of labor, and your attitudes toward friends, recreation, and personal habits which you may find irritating in each other (chapter 11). This is not meant to be an exhaustive list. You could add many other important questions, such as religious practices and political loyalties. However, I do not personally consider these tasks of marriage to be as important as your personal feelings and attitudes to each other, so I have put them last. In the past, the tendency has been to put too much stress on these practical matters. My view is that, if once you can really get your inner selves in tune with each other, you should be able to cope together with most situations you are confronted with—whereas you will never cope with anything but turn every situation into a battleground if you have not achieved inner harmony with each other.

You will notice that I have made no attempt to give you anything like a scorecard. Many marriage books include some kind of quiz with points you can score on each question and then add up, comparing your total with something like a national average. This can be interesting and useful, but I can't feel personally very enthusiastic about it. I believe it is more helpful simply to confront you with the issues we know to be important for the making of a successful marriage, ask you to discuss them seriously together, and then leave you to draw your own conclusions. I have almost always found that through this kind of process, people develop awareness of what are the promising and the threatening factors in their relationship. Indeed, almost invariably they were already instinctively aware of these things, but often had not examined their own feelings or looked at their possible implications. People who are very much in love live very intensely in the present and are not inclined to contemplate implications. But if they plan to marry, they simply must do so. High moments when you can go hand-in-hand singing into the moonlight are great. But such sweet and tender love can have no assured future unless it is anchored to the realities of everyday living in a very complicated world. This is what getting ready for marriage means.

What Have You Learned?

Well, what do you now know about your state of readiness for marriage? After all those hours of self-examination and discussion, you will be an exceptional couple indeed if you have passed all the tests with flying colors. You would hardly be human if you had not turned up some areas in which you feel poorly prepared for marriage. The experiences of self-examination and mutual evaluation you have been through should have brought those areas clearly into the open, which was what they were intended to do.

You will now need to decide together what to do about any areas of your relationship that don't measure up to your expectations. You should try to determine whether these problem areas are caused by aspects of your individual lives or of your interaction with each other that can be changed so as to make the prospect more promising. If you think the necessary changes can be made, work out a plan that can put this to the test, now or later. In doing this, you will have to consider whether this is something you can achieve by yourselves or whether you should have professional help. In general, it is sound policy to deal with your problems yourselves so long as you find you can make acceptable progress. The effort provides you with a good learning experience and enables you to develop problem-solving techniques that may help you later in other situations.

However, if by your own unaided efforts you fail to make the progress you expect and hope for, you will reach a critical point at which it is essential to act. If at the point when your own resources have not proved adequate you do not seek help, you may soon be in serious trouble, with disillusionments turning you sour and causing a deterioration of your whole relationship. It is the height of folly to let this happen and not to seek the aid of a person with specialized knowledge. A skilled counselor may be able relatively easily to see why you are failing and put you on the right track. There is no merit whatever in suffering needlessly just because you cannot bring yourself to ask for help.

Even if you have a few problems which you can't solve, either with or without help, you will not be an unusual couple. No marriage is perfect. I have had many divorced persons who later remarried tell me that the second marriage really was no better than the first, but by that time they had learned to be more tolerant, to scale down their expectations to reasonable proportions, and to make the best of what they had. Marriage partners are fallible human beings—often weak and sometimes wayward—and we have to bear and forbear. If your assets on the whole significantly exceed your liabilities and the liabilities are of such a nature that time should liquidate at least some of them, you probably have the raw materials out of which many couples have, with patience and perseverance, made good and happy marriages. As someone once put it, if you can't realize your ideal, idealize your real.

However, what if your evaluations leave you with the

definite impression that you just don't have what it takes to achieve an acceptable marriage? Then you are faced with a very difficult situation. Since subjective judgments are not always reliable, you might want to check this out with a marriage counselor. However, it is only fair to say that if you come up with the conclusion that you just aren't right for each other, your judgment is probably correct, because such a judgment doesn't come easily and runs contrary to the normal hopes of the engaged couple who tend to take a very rosy view of the situation and minimize any negative factors.

If as your counselor I have brought you to this unhappy state of mind, I offer no apologies. I hate to cause you pain and distress, but I am fully convinced that if this is your honest conclusion, it is far better to have reached it now than to have evaded it and had to face it after the marriage had taken place and possibly children had been born. It is far, far better to break a relationship than to embark on a doubtful marriage. If two people later come to the conclusion that they were right for each other after all, they can come together again with no serious harm done. In my experience, however, this is a rare event. Most people who break up tend later to be reinforced in their decision, rather than the contrary.

My expectation, however, is that most of the couples who take this book seriously and do their homework will have the potential for a good marriage. My purpose in entering into this counseling relationship with you has been to help you to take the steps that will enable you to make the very most of your potential and develop the kind of close and warm relationship that will be deeply rewarding to you both. It is this kind of experience that would be my wish for you.

Communication and Loyalty

As we take leave of each other, what all-important message can I leave with you? I have often been asked what is the one thing, above all others, that can ensure a successful marriage? I have always found this an awkward question, because there are many ingredients that contribute to success in marriage, and what is all-important for any given couple depends on their particular set of circumstances.

I asked one of my fourth-year medical students, who read the manuscript of this book and whose judgment I consider to be very sound, what I ought to stress most. His answer was that the most important issue in early marriage was communication, the need for the couple to be open and honest with each other and to keep the flow of feeling and thought moving freely between them. I have no quarrel with that judgment. As I have already pointed out, most marriages in trouble turn out to have failed primarily in this area, and the major function of marriage counseling, as I understand it, is to help the couple to clear the clogged channels and get the flow of feeling going again between them.

Yet I am not content to let that be my parting word to you. There is something else I want to stress that is perhaps more important to couples starting out in marriage. The word that best expresses it is *loyalty*.

I once wrote an article in which I said that loyalty is the acid test of a marriage, and I still think this is profoundly true. Marriage is, in the end, the coming together of two people in the quest for the deepest kind of human relationship that can be found—a full self-giving of each to the other and uniting of two lives in the closest intimacy. Not all couples wish for this, or would tolerate this. But I am speaking of marriage at its best, and marriage at its best has a tremendous appeal because it has so much to offer.

In this quest, I see loyalty as the central quality. How can love and trust be sustained without loyalty? Loyalty is the dependable devotion you give to your closest friend, to the cause you esteem above all others. It is a pledge you make to yourself that you won't let the other person down, that you won't exploit that person or take a mean advantage. It is this kind of determination to stand by each other and to work at the marriage and make it succeed that is lacking too often today and that lies, in my opinion, behind a great many of the failures. There are marriages that simply won't work, and this sad fact has to be faced in the end. But to start out in marriage with one eye on the escape hatch is no way to succeed; for marriage, as I have surely made clear by this time, is a tough, difficult undertaking, a task that will yield success only to those who put heart and soul into it.

Many years ago, I read a book on marriage by French writer André Maurois, in which he summed this up rather neatly. He spoke of the years in which young people date each other and rate each other, and then, in the fullness of time, they make their choice of the one they want to marry. Now they have reached a turning point in life. If they know what they are doing and are serious about it, they will say, "I have chosen; from now on my aim will be, not to search for someone who will please me, but to please the one I have chosen."

If two people, having chosen each other and being satisfied that their choice is a sound one, are quite determined to please each other—in the fullest and deepest sense of the word—it's rather difficult, isn't it, to imagine how they could fail?

13

Your Future as Newlyweds

*O*n the more than ten years that have passed since this book was first written, exciting new progress has been made in our understanding of the marriage relationship. Our society is now at a very curious point—marriages are failing to an extent they never did before, while at the same time marriages are succeeding as they never did before!

In the 1920s two social scientists, Robert and Helen Lynd, made a major study of a typical American community which they called Middletown. They found that the marriages there were in a very bad state. Fifty years later, another group of social scientists revisited Middletown (Muncie, Indiana) and repeated the original Lynd study. What this group found was a great improvement in the quality of today's marriages.

How could this be? The answer is that the way out of marriage today, through divorce, is so much easier that large numbers of couples are using it to escape—a possibility that didn't exist in the old days. So what we have today is a situation in which divorce is much easier for the unhappy couples; but for the couples who stay together, marriages are much better.

This great improvement in today's marriages, according to those who made the study, is due to two factors—the new companionship between men and women, and the wide development of marriage enrichment programs.

109

The Marriage Enrichment Approach

The idea of preparing couples for their first year of marriage was first developed about a generation ago. It was adopted particularly by pastors, priests, and rabbis who naturally felt a sense of responsibility for the well-being of those upon whose future life together they pronounced the divine blessing. They saw it as their obvious duty to help those couples to get ready for the task that lay before them.

Once the couple left the church or synagogue as husband and wife, however, no further help was usually offered, unless or until their marriage was in serious trouble. It was considered improper to intrude on the privacy of a recently married couple. This amounted to a kind of cultural taboo—what we sometimes call a "no-no."

Earlier in this book, I likened preparation for marriage to getting ready for a journey to Africa—a venture into unknown territory where dangerous situations might be encountered. So it made sense to learn all you could about Africa before you set off—because once you got there, the person who had instructed you would no longer be accessible.

However, at that point the comparison breaks down. The pastor or counselor who prepared you for marriage is normally still around when you settle down for your first year of living together. So why can't he or she continue to give you guidance and help? After all, the need for help becomes much greater and more urgent when you are actually having the experience than when you are planning it in advance.

Somehow this didn't occur to the helpers. It seemed to be an invasion of your privacy. The pastor could talk to you about intimate issues in your relationship, ask you questions, and offer you advice *before* you had the experience of marriage—but *not after*! It all sounds strangely illogical, doesn't it?

What we are dealing with here is a *taboo*—something

that just isn't done. And you are not supposed to ask *why* it isn't done. It has been a social custom, and as such it must be respected, whether it makes sense or not.

Taboos are usually based on earlier experience and are preserved for good reasons. But when society changes and the reasons no longer apply, the taboos don't have to be preserved. Women, for example, were once considered to be frail creatures who needed to be protected from all kinds of dangers, real and imaginary, which we now know just don't exist. So, we have abandoned the ancient customs which prevented women from developing their full personhood.

Similarly, I believe we should now abandon the idea that we can't guide and help newlyweds through their critical first year together; and since I wrote the first edition of this book, I have strongly urged this change of policy and helped to develop experimental enrichment programs with newlyweds, which have proved to be highly successful.

Recent studies have made it very clear that the first year of marriage is the critical time for most couples. Once they are settled down together, they must establish the interaction patterns that will decide how well, or how badly, they manage their future relationship. Up to the time of the wedding, they can cling to the romantic dreams which all couples have when they first fall in love with each other. But in the day-to-day life of a shared home, they must confront the reality of who they really are, and of how their ways of behaving affect each other. We now have evidence that most couples, by the sixth month after the wedding, are ready to reach out with both hands for help which they would have rejected in the premarital period. And a major study of divorced couples in Britain found that one-third of them had already been in serious trouble by the time they celebrated their first wedding anniversay.

Robert Havighurst, a famous educator, used to talk about "the teachable moment"——the critical point in life when knowledge is likely to be eagerly seized and put to use. Suppose, for example, that you were lost in a wilderness, and starving to death, when you happened to find a book that explained which of the plants around you were good to eat and which were poisonous. How you would pounce on that book, which at any other time would hardly have aroused your interest!

I have sometimes said that preparation for marriage is like teaching people to swim on a piano stool. Sure, you can learn the strokes by waving your arms and legs in the air. But the real learning—the teachable moment—begins when you get into the water, and using the right strokes can then make all the difference between sinking and keeping afloat.

In our experimental working with newlyweds, we have made some interesting discoveries. The main one is that once the couples have grasped the idea that they are at the teachable moment so far as marriage is concerned, they don't need to have their privacy protected, but would far rather have a chance to get their questions answered and their problems solved. They find it an enormous relief to be able to share their experiences with other newlyweds, because they discover that all of them are going through very similar experiences and need to learn new skills in coping with the adjustments they have to make. After going through experiences of this kind, the deep gratitude of these couples has been quite touching—almost like the gratitude of starving people to whom someone has at last given food.

Following these discoveries, I have come to see that although marriage preparation can be helpful, it is absurd to halt the process as soon as the couple get into the water. I have also come to feel that giving people "instruction" before marriage is of very limited value—and this has now been confirmed by careful research. It is now clear from a number of studies that the best kind of help for engaged couples is not to talk *to them* but to open up the way for them to talk *to each other*—about their personal lives, their hopes and fears, and the deep kinds of interpersonal realities with which they will have to struggle later, if and when they do marry.

That explains what I have tried to do in this book. Anything I have said to you is of minor value compared to what you have said to each other. And in going through the book, merely reading is not to be compared with what you can gain from using it to get into deeper touch with each other. If, of course, anything I have *said* has been of value to you, I am glad and grateful. But the real gain to you two can come only from *doing together* what I have been urging you to do.

So I would now encourage you not simply to *prepare* yourselves for marriage. That is a good thing to do. But what is far more important is how you use that critical first year when you are newlyweds. I hope you can somehow manage not to have to travel alone together on that eventful journey. Try to get into some kind of marriage enrichment group in which you can share your experiences with others and get their support and help. Or find a marriage counselor who can plan a series of monthly or bimonthly sessions with you and guide you through your first year, helping you to develop creative interaction patterns that will enable you to change and grow toward the development of your full relational potential.

And so, in closing, let me wish for you both a very happy marriage!

People Who Can Help You

*I*n this book I have tried to act as your premarital counselor without ever actually seeing you or meeting you personally.

Only you can say how far this experience has been helpful. If you feel that it has provided you with the preparation for marriage you needed, and you have not become aware of any problems you can't handle by yourselves, I am satisfied. But if you now recognize that you need some further help, I want to continue to be your counselor by showing you how you can find it. I can do this in two ways.

The first way is easy. I have prepared for you a list of books to which you can turn for further reading. Through such reading you can become students of the most distinguished authorities. The list in Appendix 2 includes a few comments about each book, so that you may have some idea of where to turn for the particular information you need.

How to Locate a Marriage Counselor

The other way of guiding you to further help is a little more difficult. It is to refer you to an actual counselor with whom you can work on some of the more knotty problems that may have come up. Fortunately there are now in most parts of the United States capable and well-trained people who can give you the help you may need. The problem is how to locate them.

One way in which we locate services of other kinds is

through the yellow pages of the telephone directory. Unfortunately this may not be a good way of finding a counselor. There are all kinds of people who call themselves "marriage and family counselors" and who list themselves as such in the yellow pages. Some are very competent people. Others, alas, are not. And it is hard to tell the difference. Often those who are least qualified print a lot of impressive material about what they have to offer and in this way draw attention to themselves—professional people are forbidden to do this by the associations to which they belong. Usually anyone with an M.D. or Ph.D. degree would be dependable. But there are many good counselors without such qualifications. For example, some social workers with M.S.W. degrees are highly skilled marriage counselors.

Any marriage counselor who indicates membership in the American Association for Marriage and Family Therapy (AAMFT, formerly the American Association of Marriage Counselors, AAMC) can be relied on, because in order to become a member of this national interprofessional organization a counselor must measure up to high standards of training, and the association has a code of professional ethics to which members must conform. In states where marriage counselors are licensed (for instance, in California, in Michigan, and in New Jersey), this qualification also means that requirements have had to be met, though they are not generally as high as those of the national organization. In some telephone directories, accredited members of these groups advertise their services together in a block listing.

If you care to take the trouble, you can write to the national headquarters of the AAMFT (1717 K Street, Suite 407, Washington, D. C. 20006) and ask for names of its members in your locality. Enclose a stamped, self-addressed envelope for the reply.

A good way to get information about local counseling services is to call one of the various agencies in your community. The local affiliate of the Family Service Association of America would be the best place to start. Your official local mental health organization would also be a good source. Another possibility is the department of psychology or the department of sociology at your local college or university.

Even when you have located a marriage counselor, you should reserve judgment about him or her until you have had an actual interview. Don't hesitate to ask questions about the counselor's qualifications and training. A competent professional will not mind this in the least. If the counselor seems to resent such inquiries, you had better be on your guard. Be particularly alert if the counselor makes grandiose claims about what he or she can do for you. If the fees are out of reach, say so frankly and ask for suggestions about how you can get help at a price you can afford. If after one or two interviews you just don't feel confidence in the counselor and you don't seem to be getting the help you need, you don't have to stay with this person.

Now let me offer some general comments about other professional people, not necessarily specialists in marriage counseling, whose help you might seek.

Your Pastor

In all matters relating to preparation for marriage, your pastor is likely to be your best friend, and you would be wise to discuss with him anything you plan to do. Pastors conduct weddings, and they are well aware of the importance of adequate preparation for the adjustments of married life. There is little doubt that pastors, priests, and rabbis undertake far more marriage preparation than all members of the other professions combined.

Many pastors routinely invite the couple to meet with them before the wedding. Some have been thoroughly trained in premarital counseling and do an excellent job. Others, lacking training, do their best, but it isn't as thorough as they would wish. One of my hopes is that some pastors may find it helpful to use this book as a means of venturing further into the field than they have done before and of giving better service to their young people.

Your pastor will, of course, go over the wedding service

with you in advance and interpret to you just what it means, and will also probably set up a wedding rehearsal. By these means you will be set free from needless anxiety or uncertainty about how to act when the time comes. This should enable you to participate wholeheartedly in the ritual, making the wedding a happy and memorable occasion, as it should be.

Apart from the wedding ceremony, your pastor can be a good friend to you in the process of leaving your parental home and setting up your own new home. Churches in these days are becoming more and more family-centered in their emphasis. Don't hesitate to turn to your pastor for any help you may need, now or later, as you venture forth into the state of matrimony.

Your Physician

Physicians in general don't have the same close contact as pastors do with people about to marry. It is true that in most states it is necessary for the future husband and wife to take a blood test and sometimes to meet other health requirements. But usually you go to a center where you see only the receptionist and the laboratory technician who takes the blood sample, without ever meeting the physician in charge.

A number of questions arise, however, about which a physician's help may be needed before marriage. Let me refer to some of these:

1. *General examination.* Some people think it is a good plan, before marriage, for both partners to have a complete physical checkup, and to "exchange health certificates." Marriage involves the sharing of life, and the reasoning is that if you are taking each other "for better or worse," each of you should know the medical outlook for the other as it is interpreted by a physician. This is obvious in cases where one partner has some disease or disability which reduces or hinders the capacity to live a normal life, but there may also be factors in a person's physical makeup which, while not now interfering with normal functioning, could do so later.

By putting all the cards on the table now, you can avoid any possible misunderstanding or recrimination later. This makes good sense.

2. *Genital examination*. Many women go to a gynecologist for a checkup prior to marriage. The physician can quickly identify any condition of the sex organs that might need attention. If the woman is a virgin, she may possibly have a resistant hymen that will not stretch or break easily, and this could spoil the honeymoon by making penetration by the penis impossible. The physician can deal with the trouble very simply, using only a local anesthetic. Other malformations of the female sex organs (fortunately these are quite rare) can be recognized and dealt with.

The usual purpose of her visit to her physician, however, is in order to get advice and help about birth control. When the diaphragm was the most widely used method, a fitting was required. The pill at present has to be prescribed by a physician, and the I.U.D. (intrauterine device) put in place by a physician. So birth control is still, for most women, the primary service for which they turn to their doctors.

A genital examination is not normally required for the husband-to-be. Unless obvious abnormalities of the sex organ are present, the physician cannot make any reliable predictions about its capacity to function. Problems of male sex adjustment are in the great majority of cases emotional in origin.

3. *Sex techniques*. Both partners sometimes seek a consultation with their physician in order to ensure that their sex education is adequate, and particularly to talk over sexual anxieties and uncertainties. All physicians are not equally well equipped to give this kind of help, but some who have specialized in the field can be the best possible counselors and can give the couple help and reassurance that should be of great value to them. Those who are not inclined to do this kind of counseling themselves can usually refer the couple to someone who will do so.

4. *Genetic examination*. Occasionally a couple, sure that they want to marry each other, are not equally sure that they ought to have children, because in the family background of one or of both there is evidence of inherited disease or defect.

Anxieties of this kind can be distressing, and it is a wise plan to get the expert opinion of a specialist in genetics. Considerable progress has been made in recent years in the understanding of these inherited conditions, and we are now able to make some fairly accurate predictions which can help a couple to estimate the percentage of risk that children born to them would suffer from inherited disability. Your regular physician can refer you to a geneticist.

Other Professional Helpers

The basic members of the marriage preparation team are the marriage counselor, the pastor, and the physician. You should not hesitate to seek their advice and cooperation. Getting married, as some of the wedding rituals remind us, is a highly responsible undertaking, not to be embarked upon lightly or irresponsibly. The success of your marriage is a matter far too important to leave to chance, and when there are people in your community whose assistance could make all the difference between success or failure, between happiness and misery, it is folly not to seek that help and to make use of it.

Additional helpers can be sought when special needs must be met. Personality problems are best handled by the clinical psychologist or the psychiatrist. Legal difficulties obviously lie in the sphere of the lawyer, and this is no place for do-it-yourself efforts. Financial tangles also call for expert guidance, and your bank should be able to put you in touch with someone who can provide this.

Modern social workers are often very versatile people, and the staff of a family service agency often includes men and women with a wide variety of specialized skills. It is in fact surprising and reassuring to investigate the impressive array of services which modern American communities provide to help people, covering almost every conceivable kind of human need. Few of these services existed a generation ago. Many of them still do not exist in other countries. You are fortunate to be living in a land so rich in resources. It is your privilege to make good use of them.

Appendix 2

Books for Your Further Reading

*I*f you were about to launch a new career, in which you had no previous experience, or which you had previously attempted without success, what would be the obvious thing to do?

You know the answer. You would want to learn all you could from people who have knowledge and experience.

How would you do this? The simplest way would be to read the books these people have written. Publishers as a rule don't print books by people who don't know what they're talking about.

Well, *are* there books that can give you reliable information about how to make a marriage work? Yes, there are. But how do you find them?

I'm going to challenge both of you, quite seriously, as a basic part of your "getting ready for marriage," to read at least three books, and better six books. And I'm going to give you a list, carefully selected, to choose from.

I have personally read most of these books, and I consider that they can provide helpful guidance for any couple who are taking marriage seriously. And anyone who is *not* taking it seriously, at a time when half of all new marriages are likely to end in failure, is simply irresponsible.

My list is confined to books written for the average couple. I have deliberately left out some otherwise excellent books, because they are technical or complicated. The ones I have picked are quite short, and they should take only a few hours to go through. But they do discuss issues that may be vital to your future happiness.

Suppose you agree to read six books, and devote four hours to each. That's a total of twenty-four hours—equal to one day of your life. Of course you would want to space the reading out over a few weeks. But even so, that's a very small investment toward a happy marriage, isn't it?

Here's what to do. Just take the list to a library or bookstore. You have plenty of titles to choose from, so you should be able to find some of them. I suggest that you make notes as you read, and then talk together about points of special interest or concern. Also, many of today's books on marriage provide exercises for couples to do together.

If you read as many as six books, you should find answers to most of your questions. And you may even be able to give good advice to some of your friends! Doesn't this make sense?

I have listed the books alphabetically by name of author, with publisher and date, and a brief description.

How did I select these books? I went carefully through my library with you in mind. I ended up with over eighty books. Yes, over eighty! Did you know there were as many as that? There are more, in fact, because there must be others that I don't know about.

I decided that I must cut down the number, and I settled for a total of fifty. I began by leaving out all books published before the year 1970. That included two of my own earlier books—but never mind, we have learned a lot about marriage since the older books were written. Also, I removed from the list any books that were technical or very long, and therefore not easy to read. Most of those that were left are short and chatty, with plenty of stories about people, real or imaginary. They are written for the average couple, and each should take only a few hours to go through. They talk about issues that may be vital for your future happiness.

Let me conclude with some wise words that Herbert Newton once spoke: "The dignity of a career must always be measured by the seriousness of the preparation made for it. How then do we value marriage?"

The List of Books

Achtemeier, Elizabeth. *The Committed Marriage*. Philadelphia: The Westminster Press, 1976. What Christian marriage means in our contemporary culture.

Bower, Robert. *Solving Problems in Marriage*. Grand Rapids: Wm. B. Eerdmans Publishing Co., 1972. Guidance on how to deal with relational stress and conflict.

Broderick, Carlfred. *Couples: How to Confront Problems and Maintain Loving Relationships*. New York: Simon & Schuster, 1979. A distinguished family professional helps couples to cope.

Brothers, Joyce. *The Brothers System for Liberated Love and Marriage*. Ridgefield, Conn.: Wyden Books, 1972. A collection of "ideas that work," by a well-known psychologist.

Bry, Adelaide, and Leonard Felder. *Learning to Love Forever*. New York: Macmillan, 1982. A forty-day program for a couple to follow, with daily exercises.

Calden, George. *I Count—You Count*. Niles, Ill.: Argus Communications, 1976. Exercises and activities for individual couples, or a group of couples, to use for marriage enrichment.

Campbell, Susan. *The Couples' Journey: Intimacy as a Path to Wholeness*. San Luis Obispo, Calif.: Impact Publishers, 1980. A clinical psychologist describes marriage as a journey with five stages.

Cameron-Bandler, Leslie. *They Lived Happily Ever After*. Cupertino, Calif.: Meta Publications, 1978. A book about how to do it.

Cicero, Jim and June, and Ivan and Joyce Fahs. *Conversations on Sex and Love in Marriage*. Waco, Tex.: Word, 1972. A book of honest dialogues by two Christian couples.

Clinebell, Howard and Charlotte. *The Intimate Marriage*. New

York: Harper & Row, 1970. An older book, but one which helped to open up the new field of marriage enrichment.

Denton, Wallace and Juanita. *Creative Couples—The Growth Factor in Marriage*. Philadelphia: The Westminster Press, 1983. A challenging message that sees couples capable of almost unlimited growth.

Dufresne, Edward. *Partnership: Marriage and the Committed Life*. Ramsey, N.J.: Paulist Press, 1975. How to achieve a Christian marriage in today's world.

Edens, David. *Marriage: How to Have It the Way You Want It*. Englewood Cliffs, N.J.: Prentice-Hall, 1982. A readable book by a very successful college teacher of family courses.

Erdahl, Lowell and Carol. *Be Good to Each Other: An Open Letter on Marriage*. New York: Hawthorn Books, 1976. A happily married couple share their experience with a young couple starting out.

Fairfield, James. *When You Don't Agree*. Scottdale, Penn.: Herald Press, 1977. A detailed account of how to resolve marriage and family conflicts.

Ford, Edward. *Choosing to Love: A New Way to Respond*. Minneapolis: Winston Press, 1983. A marriage counselor shares his wide experience with couples who take their relationship seriously.

Garrett, Yvonne. *The Newlywed Handbook*. Waco, Tex.: Word, 1981. A wife, thirty-five years married, has run a class for newlyweds and writes about critical issues that occur in early marriage.

Grace, Mike and Joyce. *A Joyful Meeting: Sexuality in Marriage*. St. Paul: National Marriage Encounter, 1980. An unusually helpful book on a subject about which much has been written.

Hall, Douglas and Francine. *The Two-Career Couple*. Reading, Mass.: Addison-Wesley, 1979. A good account of how to manage when both partners work outside the home.

Hardisty, Margaret. *Forever My Love—What Every Man Should Know About His Wife*. Eugene, Ore.: Harvest House Publishers, 1975. An attorney's wife grapples with the question in a lively style.

Hart, Kathleen and Thomas. *The First Two Years of Marriage*. Ramsey, N.J.: Paulist Press, 1983. A realistic and convincing appraisal of how to establish a good relationship.

James, Muriel. *Marriage Is for Loving*. Reading, Mass.: Addison-Wesley, 1979. A book aimed at helping couples to achieve good relationships.

Jones, Ruth Ann and William. *Living in Love: A Guide to Realistic Christian Marriage*. Atlanta: John Knox Press, 1977. A couple dialogue about nine areas of marriage and how to manage them.

Keyes, Margaret. *Staying Married*. Millbrae, Calif.: Les Femmes, 1975. Full of encouragement and practical ideas for couples willing to work at their marriages.

Kilgore, James. *Try Marriage Before Divorce*. Waco, Tex.: Word, 1978. A well-known marriage counselor provides a month's program to encourage couples to take their marriage seriously.

Kranzler, Mel. *Creative Marriage*. New York: McGraw-Hill, 1981. The author believes that "marriage is one area in modern life in which every couple has the total power to shape its course." This very positive view is explained and emphasized.

Landorf, Joyce. *Tough and Tender: What Every Woman Wants in a Man*. Old Tappan, N.J.: Fleming Revell, 1975. A popular religious woman talks about desirable qualities in a husband.

Langsdale, Richard. *Getting Ready for Living Together*. Philadelphia: Fortress Press, 1974. A Lutheran pastor offers help in the task of marriage building.

Larson, Ronald and Doris. *I Need to Have You Know Me: Guide to a Better Marriage.* Minneapolis: Winston Press, 1981. A book of exercises for couples to do separately and then share, as a means of improving communication.

Liontos, Lynn and Demetri. *The Good Couple Life.* Eugene, Ore.: Guard, 1982. A twelve-month guide to the first year of marriage, full of practical wisdom.

Mace, David and Vera. *How to Have a Happy Marriage.* Nashville: Abingdon Press, 1977. A six-week enrichment program for married couples, tested and proved effective.

Miller, Sherod, et al. *Straight Talk: A New Way to Get Closer to Others by Saying What You Really Mean.* New York: Rawson, Wade, 1981. A readable account of a pioneering program for couple communication training.

Molton, Warren. *Friends, Partners, and Lovers: A Good Word About Marriage.* Valley Forge, Penn.: Judson Press, 1979. A gifted counselor talks sensitively about the joys and fulfillment of marriage. Another book of his is *Spheres of Intimacy*, Pinion, 1982.

O'Brien, Patricia. *Staying Together.* New York: Random House, 1977. How to deal creatively with your differences and disagreements.

Osborne, Cecil. *The Art of Understanding Your Mate.* Grand Rapids: The Zondervan Corp., 1979. All about the adjustments of married life.

Paul, Jordan and Margaret. *Free to Love: Creating and Sustaining Intimacy in Marriage.* New York: Hawthorn Books, 1975. A first-hand account of a couple's marital growth.

Powell, John. *The Secret of Staying in Love.* Niles, Ill.: Argus Communications, 1974. Written by a distinguished Catholic priest, this book has been a very popular one.

Quesnell, John. *Marriage: A Discovery Together.* South Bend, Ind.: Fides Claretian, 1974. A Catholic counselor tries to reconcile traditional Christian values with modern marriage.

Ryan, Kevin and Marilyn. *Making a Marriage.* New York: St. Martin's Press, 1982. A couple share their experience of building a fulfilling relationship.

Rogers, Carl. *Becoming Partners.* New York: Delacorte Press, 1972. A distinguished psychologist talks about close relationships.

Rosenman, Martin. *Loving Styles: A Guide for Increasing Intimacy.* Englewood Cliffs, N.J.:Prentice-Hall, 1979. A psychologist explains how love can be enhanced in marriage.

Samuel, Dorothy. *Love, Liberation, and Marriage.* New York: Funk & Wagnalls, 1976. How liberated women can still make marriage work.

Southard, Samuel. *Like the One You Love.* Philadelphia: The Westminster Press, 1974. A discussion of intimacy and equality in modern mariage.

Stapleton, Jean, and Richard Bright. *Equal Marriage.* Nashville: Abingdon Press, 1976. A modern couple discuss their concept of equality.

Swain, Clark. *Enriching Your Marriage: A Tune-up for Partners in Love.* New York: Horizon Press, 1982. A very readable book for "all people who have the courage to commit themselves to better living and better loving."

Thatcher, Floyd and Harriet. *Long Term Marriage: A Search for the Ingredients of a Life-time Partnership.* Waco, Tex.: Word, 1980. The findings of an inquiry in which more than a hundred married couples were interviewed.

Travis, Robert and Patricia. *Vitalizing Intimacy in Marriage.* Chicago: Nelson-Hall Publishers, 1979. Teachers in a medical school, who developed the Pairing Intimacy Program, share what they have learned.

Weise, Bernard, and Urban Steinmetz. *Everything You Need to Know to Stay Married and Like It.* Grand Rapids: The

Zondervan Corp., 1972. *Some* things worth knowing anyway!

Wilke, Richard. *Tell Me Again, I'm Listening.* Nashville: Abingdon Press, 1973. Effective communication is explained and taught as the foundation of successful marriage.

Yancey, Philip. *After the Wedding.* Waco, Tex.: Word, 1976. Nine Christian couples tell how they got through their first five years of marriage.

cover photograph Sid Dorris
cover & book design Steve Laughbaum
models for cover photograph Karen Trogdon & Randall Butler